Series/Number 07-134

# GENERALIZED LINEAR MODELS: A UNIFIED APPROACH

**JEFF GILL**
*University of Florida*

D1113308

**Sage** PUBLICATIONS
*International Educational and Professional Publisher*
Thousand Oaks  London  New Delhi

*ADI–5014*

Copyright © 2001 by Sage Publications, Inc.

*For information:*

SAGE Publications, Inc.
2455 Teller Road
Thousand Oaks, California 91320
E-mail: order@sagepub.com

Sage Publications Ltd.
6 Bonhill Street
London EC2A 4PU
United Kingdom

Sage Publications India Pvt. Ltd.
M-32 Market
Greater Kailash I
New Delhi 110 048 India

Printed in the United States of America

ISBN 0-7619-2055-2 (pbk.: acid-free paper)

This book is printed on acid-free paper.

00   01   02   03   04   05   06   7   6   5   4   3   2   1

QA
276
.G455
2001

| | |
|---|---|
| *Acquiring Editor:* | C. Deborah Laughton |
| *Editorial Assistant:* | Eileen Carr |
| *Production Editor:* | Sanford Robinson |
| *Production Assistant:* | Victoria Cheng |
| *Typesetter:* | Technical Typesetting Inc. |

When citing a university paper, please use the proper form. Remember to cite the Sage University Paper series title and include the paper number. One of the following formats can be adapted (depending on the style manual used):

(1) GILL, J. (2000) *Generalized Linear Models: A Unified Approach*. Sage University Papers Series on Quantitative Applications in the Social Sciences, 07-134. Thousand Oaks, CA: Sage.

OR

(2) Gill, J. (2000). *Generalized Linear Models: A Unified Approach*. (Sage University Papers Series on Quantitative Applications in the Social Sciences, series no. 07-134). Thousand Oaks, CA: Sage.

# CONTENTS

## ACKNOWLEDGMENTS

I thank my reviewers, Scott R. Eliason from the Department of Sociology, University of Iowa, Iowa City, IA 52242-1401 for Review A, William Berry from the Department of Political Science, Florida State University, Tallahassee, FL 32306-2049 for Review B, and B. Dan Wood from the Department of Political Science, Texas A&M University, College Station, TX 77843-4348. I also thank Brad Palmquist, Kevin Kerr, and the Boston Chapter of the American Statistical Association.

## SERIES EDITOR'S INTRODUCTION

The basic linear model estimated by ordinary least squares (OLS) regression makes a good first cut at the data, but may not make a good last cut. The Gauss–Markov assumptions upon which it rests are powerful in concept, but demanding in practice. On the one hand, if the dependent variable is skewed or categorical, the analyst might turn from OLS to logit estimation. (In this series, see DeMaris, *Logit Modeling*, No. 85; Hagenaars, *Loglinear Models with Latent Variables*, No. 94; Ishii-Kuntz, *Ordinal Log-Linear Models*, No. 97; Menard, *Applied Logistic Regression Analysis*, No. 106). On the other hand, the analyst might resort to probit, and so consult the monographs which make that comparison (Aldrich and Nelson, *Linear Probability, Logit, and Probit Models*, No. 45; Liao, *Interpreting Probability Models*, No. 101). Still differently, perhaps the variables are censored, or consist of event counts, in which case the monographs by Breen (*Regression Models: Censored, Sample Selected or Truncated Data*, No. 111) and (Allison, *Event History Analysis*, No. 46) merit more attention.

These departures from OLS are well and good. The problem is that they are piecemeal. Each assumption violation receives treatment in isolation, with special procedures. Lost is the interconnection of the issues and the methods. However, here Professor Gill offers a unified approach in the *generalized linear model*, which subsumes the basic linear model, as well as logit and other probability models. First, common probability density and probability mass functions are brought under one roof, as the exponential family. Then, the maximum likelihood function for that family of distributions is developed. After this setup, in what constitutes the heart of the monograph (Chapter 4), the linear model is generalized by means of a link function compatible with discrete, bounded dependent variables.

With regard to software, most standard packages now support generalized linear models, and its computational technique of iterative weighted least squares (IWLS). To illustrate the application of IWLS and the interpretation of the coefficients, the author provides numerous original modeling exercises on real world social science data. He examines the following questions: capital punishment in the American states; a taxation vote for the new Scottish parliament; standardized educational testing in California; the assignment of bills to congressional committees; the world copper price. Such a wide variety gives the reader a good feel for the results generated by the method.

In generalized linear modeling, issues of residual behavior and model fit are as important as they are with basic linear modeling, although arriving at accepted performance benchmarks is more difficult. While these residuals are commonly not normally distributed, normality still remains a useful diagnostic standard. Five different kinds of residuals are available for examination: response, Pearson, working, Anscombe, and deviance. According to Dr. Gill, the deviance residual is the most useful. Turning to goodness of fit, there are also five choices: the chi-square approximation, the Akaike information criterion, the Schwartz criterion; graphs, and the summed deviance statistic (which the author is partial to).

In social science research, the principle of Occam's razor—parsimony—has high value. The usual assumptions of OLS are few and have taken analysts far. However, interval measurement and normality requirements can be barriers on the road. Generalized linear modeling, carefully articulated by Professor Gill, helps remove those barriers and, at the same time, preserve the parsimony principle.

—Michael S. Lewis-Beck
Series Editor

# GENERALIZED LINEAR MODELS: A UNIFIED APPROACH

**JEFF GILL**
*University of Florida*

## 1. INTRODUCTION

Social scientists employ a vast array of data-analytic techniques to explore and explain various empirical phenomenon. Many, if not most, of these tools are imported wholesale from applied statistics. This has been a productive research strategy since a large number of the problems encountered by social science researchers can be solved by well-developed and readily available statistical methodologies. Unfortunately, it is sometimes the case that in this diffusion of intellectual material, techniques are unnecessarily treated as distinct and particular. This is certainly true of class of regression techniques that include: logit and probit regression, truncated distribution models, event count models, probability outcome models, and the basic linear model. All of these (and more) are actually special cases of the *Generalized Linear Model*: a single methodology for producing model parameter estimates.

A typical social science graduate methodological education starts with learning the linear model (actually this is where some cases also *end*), followed by an introduction to discrete choice models, survival models, counting models, and perhaps more. This leads to a very compartmented and necessarily limited view of the world. It also means that a multitude of special procedures, specifications, and diagnostics must be learned separately. Conversely, the approach taken in this monograph is to see all of these approaches as special cases of one generalized procedure. Therefore, the material in this work complements other texts by tying together and synthesizing seemingly distinct tools.

This monograph explains and demonstrates a *unified approach* to applying regression models in the social sciences. Once the general framework is understood, then the appropriate choice of model configuration is determined simply by the structure of the outcome variable and the nature of the dispersion. This process not only leads to a better understanding of the theoretical basis of the model, but also increases the researcher's flexibility with regard to new data types.

The basic principle behind the generalized linear model is that the systematic component of the linear model can be transformed to create an analytical framework that closely resembles the standard linear model but accommodates a wide variety of nonnormal and noninterval measured outcome variables. The Gauss–Markov assumptions that underlie linear model theory require that the error component be distributed independently with mean zero and constant variance. If the outcome variable is drawn from a nonnormal distribution, then these assumptions often cannot be met and serious errors of estimation efficiency occur, although the linear model is robust to mild deviations. Generalized linear models employ a "link function" which defines the relationship between the systematic component of the data and the outcome variable in such a way that asymptotic normality and constancy of variance are no longer required. However, it is still important to be able to assume uncorrelated observations. This allows the creation of a wide class of models loosened from the restrictions of standard linear theory.

To unify seemingly diverse probabilistic forms, the generalized approach first recasts common probability density functions and probability mass functions into a consolidated exponential family form. This facilitates the development of a more rigorous and thorough theoretical treatment of the principles underlying transformationally developed linear models. The first unifying treatment by Nelder and Wedderburn (1972) demonstrated that an understanding of the results from applied statistical work can be greatly enhanced by this further development of the general theory.

The approach taken here emphasizes the *theoretical* foundations of the generalized linear model rather than a laundry list of applications. As a result, most of the effort will be spent on the mathematical statistical theory that supports this construct. Several familiar distributions are developed as examples, but the emphasis on theory means that readers will be able to develop an appropriate generalized linear model specification for their own data-analytic applications.

## Model Specification

George Box is purported to have said "All models are wrong. Some are useful." This is an observation that developing statistical models is necessarily a simplification and a reduction in supplied information. Model specification is a process of determining what features of the data are important and what features need not be reported. This activity focuses on determining which explanatory variables to include and which to ignore, positing a mathematical and probabilistic relationship between the explanatory variables and the outcome variable, and establishing some criteria for success. Model specification and implementation produce summary statistics which are hopefully sufficient in the statistical and colloquial sense for unknown population parameters of interest.

Model specification is really more art than science in that a huge number of possible specifications can be developed from even a modest set of factors.[1] Generally the researcher has a theoretical justification for some subset of specifications, and in most fields there are conventions about variable inclusion. At the foundation of this process is a trade-off between parsimony and fit. Specifying parsimonious models is efficient in that less important effects are ignored. Such models are often highly generalizable because the conditions of applicability are more easily obtained (wide scope). However, the more simple the model becomes, the extreme being describing all outcome variable behavior by the mean $\mu$, the greater the probability that the error term contains important systematic information, holding all other considerations constant. In the worst case, this leads to biased estimators. Also, whenever there is *any* stochastic component to the model, whether it leads to bias or not, the model is literally wrong in the Box sense mentioned previously.

We can also develop a model that is completely correct though limited in its ability to describe the underlying structure of the data. Such a model, called saturated or full, is essentially a set of parameters equal to the number of data points, each indexed by an indicator function. So every parameter is exactly correct since it perfectly describes the location of an observed data point. However, this model provides no data reduction and has limited inferential value.[2] Saturated models are tremendously useful heuristic devices that allow us to benchmark hypothesized model specifications (cf. Lindsey, 1997, pp. 214–215, and Neter, Kutner, Nachtsheim, & Wasserman,

1996, pp. 586–587). Later it will be shown that the saturated model is required to create a residual-like deviance for assessing the quality of fit for a tested specification. Typical statistical models differ from saturated models in that they are an attempt to reduce the size and complexity of an observed set of data down to a small number of summary statistics. These models trade certainty for greater simplicity by making *inferential* claims about underlying population values. The estimated parameter values from this procedure are quite literally wrong, but by providing the associated level of uncertainty the degree of *reliability* is assessed.

In general, the purpose of model specification is to develop $\hat{\mathbf{Y}}$, a set of fitted values from the model that closely resembles the observed outcome variable values, $\mathbf{Y}$. The closer $\hat{\mathbf{Y}}$ is to $\mathbf{Y}$, the more we feel that our model accurately describes reality. However, this goal is not solitary or we would simply be content with the saturated model. Thus, a good model balances the competing objectives of parsimony and fit.

Generalized linear models do not differ in any important way from regular linear models in terms of the process of model specification except that a link function is included to accommodate noncontinuous and possibly bounded outcome variables. Therefore, all of the admonitions about the dangers of data mining, star-gazing, inverse probability misinterpretation, and probabilistic theory confirmation apply (Gill, 1999; Greenwald, 1975; Leamer, 1978; Lindsay, 1995; Miller, 1990; Rozeboom, 1960). It is also important to be aware that a single data set can lead to many perfectly plausible model specifications and subsequent substantive conclusions (Raftery, 1995).

Some important restrictions should be noted. Generalized linear models require uncorrelated cases. Time series and spatial problems can be accommodated but not without additional and sometimes complicated enhancements. Also, there can be only one error term specified in the model. While the distribution of this error term is no longer required to be asymptotically normal with constant variance (as in the linear model), approaches such as cell means models with "stacked" error terms are excluded in the basic framework. Finally, generalized linear models are inherently *parametric* in that the form of the likelihood function is completely defined by the researcher. Relaxation of this requirement through the use of smoothers leads to the more flexible but more complicated form referred to as generalized *additive* models (Hastie & Tibshirani, 1990).

**Prerequisites and Preliminaries**

*Probability Distributions*

Distributions of random variables are described by their *probability mass functions* (discrete case, PMF) or their *probability density functions* (continuous case, PDF). Probability mass functions and probability density functions are just probabilistic statements (probability *functions* specifically) about the distribution of some random variable, $Y$, over a defined range (support). In the discrete case it is denoted $P(Y = y)$ for the probability that the random variable $Y$ takes on some realization $y$, and in the continuous case we just use $f(y)$. If the random variable is conditioned on known or unknown terms, then it is common to be explicit about this relationship in the notation. For example, the distribution of a normal random variable is conditioned on the population mean ($\mu$) and variance ($\sigma^2$), and is thus denoted $f(y|\mu, \sigma^2)$.

*Example 1.1: Uniform Distributions over the Unit Interval.* A variable that is uniformly distributed over $[0, 1]$ has the probability function,

k-category discrete case (PMF):  continuous case (PDF):

$$P(Y=y)=\begin{cases} \frac{1}{k}, & \text{for } y=1,2,\ldots,k \\ 0, & \text{otherwise} \end{cases} \quad f(y)=\begin{cases} \frac{1}{b-a}, & \text{for } a=0\leq y \\ & \leq b=1 \\ 0, & \text{otherwise} \end{cases}.$$

$$(1.1)$$

There is no ambiguity here; a uniform random variable over $[0, 1]$ can be discrete, or it can be continuous. A discrete example is the coding of the outcome of the toss of a fair coin, and a continuous example is perhaps the unconditional probability of a judicial decision. The essential requirement is that the specified PMF or PDF describe the characteristics of the data generation process: bounds and differences in probabilities. The uniform distribution is useful when describing equal probability events over some unknown range ($[0, 1]$ in this case).

There are some mathematical necessities required for probability functions to be well defined. Probability distributions must be defined with regard to some *measure*, i.e., specified over some measure space. This means that a probability function has no meaning except with regard to a measure of the space to which it is applied so that there is some structure on the set of outcomes. Define a $\sigma$-algebra as a class of outcomes that includes (1) the full sample space (all possible outcomes), (2) the compliment of any included outcome, and (3) the property that the union of any countable collection of outcomes is also included. A *measure* is a function that assigns nonnegative values to outcomes and collections of outcomes in the $\sigma$-algebra. The classic example of a measure is the *Lebesgue measure*: some specified $k$-dimensional finite Euclidean space in which specific subregions can be uniquely identified. Another germane measure is the *counting measure* which is simply the set of integers from zero to infinity or some specified limit. Thus, these measures characterize the way outcomes are treated probabilistically.

Greatly simplified, a probability function on a given measure has the requirements that something must happen with probability one, nothing happens with probability zero, and the sum of the probability of disjoint events is equal to the probability of the union of these events. Furthermore probabilities are bounded by zero and one over this measure and any event outside of the measure has probability zero of occurrence. This theoretical "tidying up" is necessary to avoid pathologies such as negative probabilities and incomplete sample spaces. It is also required that PMFs sum to one and PDFs integrate to one (thus termed "proper"). Violation of this stipulation is equivalent to saying that the probability function uniformly underestimates or overestimates the probability of occurrences.

I will often talk of a *family* of distributions to indicate that parameterizations alter the characteristics of the probability function. For instance the Gaussian-normal family of distributions is a familiar set of unimodal symmetric distributions which vary by location, determined by $\mu$, and dispersion or scale, determined by $\sigma^2$. The idea of a family is very useful because it reminds us that these are mathematically similar forms which change only by altering specified parameter values. In particular, I will focus on the *exponential family* of distributions in the development of generalized linear models.

## The Linear Model

It is assumed that the reader is familiar with the multiple regression linear model in matrix notation summarized by

$$\mathbf{Y} = \mathbf{X}\boldsymbol{\beta} + \boldsymbol{\epsilon}, \tag{1.2}$$

where **Y** is an $n \times 1$ column vector containing the outcome variable, **X** is an $n \times k$ matrix of explanatory variables with rank $k$ and a leading column vector of ones, **β** is a $k \times 1$ column vector of estimated coefficients, and **ε** is a $n \times 1$ column vector of disturbances. On the right-hand side, **Xβ** is called the systematic component and **ε** is called the stochastic component.

As the name implies, generalized linear models are built on the framework of the classic linear model which dates back to the 19th century (Gauss and Legendre). The linear model, as elegant as it is, requires a relatively strict set of assumptions. The Gauss–Markov theorem states that if:

1. the relationship between each explanatory variable and the outcome variable is approximately linear in structure,
2. the residuals are independent with mean zero and constant variance,
3. there is no correlation between any regressor and disturbance,

then the solution produced by selecting coefficient values that minimize the sum of the squared residuals is unbiased and has the lowest total variance among unbiased linear alternatives. The first two restrictions are eliminated with the basic generalized linear model approach and the third can be relaxed with more advanced forms. However, the dependence of the variance on the mean function must be known (except in the extension based on quasi-likelihood functions). Generalized linear models provide a way to analyze the effects of explanatory variables in a way that closely resembles that of analyzing covariates in a standard linear model, except that the assumptions are far less confining. The key is the specification of a *link function* which links the systematic component of the linear model (**Xβ**) with a wider class outcome variables and residual forms.

### Linear Algebra and Calculus

Models and results will be discussed in matrix notation, but no linear algebra beyond Greene (2000, Chap. 1), or the first half of an introductory undergraduate linear algebra text is required. Some limited calculus knowledge is quite helpful to understanding the theoretical underpinnings of the generalized linear model. This monograph will assume familiarity with calculus at roughly the level of Kleppner and Ramsey's (1985) *Quick Calculus* or more generally

8

a first semester course. The discussion remains useful to someone without calculus knowledge with the sole exception that some of the derivations would be difficult to follow.

## Software

Understanding generalized linear models is not necessarily useful without the means of applying this understanding in practice. Consequently, software, scripts, supporting documentation, data for the examples, and some extended mathematical derivations are available freely at the author's webpage: http://web.clas.ufl.edu/~jgill. Resources and worked examples are included for several general purpose and programming environment packages: Splus, R, Gauss, SAS, SPSS, Stata, and LIMDEP.

Originally GLIM (*Generalized Linear Interactive Modeling*, Baker & Nelder, 1978) was the only package that supported generalized linear models and incorporated the associated numerical technique: *iterative weighted least squares*. However, virtually every popular package now has appropriate routines. Nonetheless, the effect that GLIM had on the development of generalized linear models was enormous. Since widespread use of the latest version, GLIM 4, has faded considerably, software support is not included on the author's webpage.

## Looking Forward

The plan of this monograph is as follows. I begin with a detailed discussion of the exponential family of distributions. This is important because the basic setup of generalized linear models applies only to parametric forms that fit this category. Next, the likelihood function for the common exponential family is derived, and from this we produce the mean and variance functions. The unified approach is apparent here because regardless of the original form of the probability function, the moments are derived in exactly the same manner. The next section introduces the linear structure and the link function which allows the generalization to take place. This idea represents the core of the theory. The computational estimation procedure for generalized linear models is introduced, and finally residuals and model fit are discussed in detail. Throughout, examples are provided as practical illustrations of applying the generalized linear model to actual data.

## 2. THE EXPONENTIAL FAMILY

The development of the theory of the generalized linear model is based upon the exponential family of distributions.[3] This formalization simply recharacterizes familiar functions into a formula that is more useful theoretically and demonstrates similarity between seemingly disparate mathematical forms. It should be noted that the exponential family form refers to a *method* in which all of the terms in the expression for these PDFs and PMFs are moved into the exponent to provide common notation. This does not imply some restrictive relationship with the well-known exponential probability density function. While generalized linear models require that the parameterization specification be restricted to cases that can be transformed to this exponential family form, it is done purely for computational reasons.

### Justification

Fisher (1934) developed the idea that many commonly applied probability mass functions and probability density functions are really just special cases of a more general classification he called the exponential family. The basic idea is to identify a general mathematical structure to the function in which uniformly labeled subfunctions characterize individual differences. The label "exponential family" comes from the convention that subfunctions are contained within the exponent component of the natural exponential function (i.e., the irrational number $e = 2.718281\ldots$ raised to some specified power). This is not a rigid restriction as any subfunction that is not in the exponent can be placed there by substituting its natural logarithm.

The primary payoff to reparameterizing a common and familiar function into the exponential form is that the isolated subfunctions quite naturally produce a small number of statistics which compactly summarize even large data sets without any loss of information. Specifically, the exponential family form readily yields sufficient statistics for the unknown parameters. A sufficient statistic for some parameter is one which contains all of the information available in a given data set about the parameter. For example, if we are interested in estimating the true range, $[a, b]$, for some uniformly distributed random variable (Example 1.1, but generalizing the bounds): $X_i \in [a, b] \forall X_i$. Then a sufficient statistic is the vector containing the first and last order statistics: $[x_{(1)}, x_{(n)}]$ from the sample of size $n$ (i.e., the smallest and largest of the sampled values). No other elements of the data and no other statistic that we could construct from the data would provide further information about the limits. Therefore $[x_{(1)}, x_{(n)}]$ provides "sufficient" information about the unknown parameters from the given data.

It has been shown (Barndorff-Nielsen, 1978, p. 114) that exponential family probability functions have all of their moments. The $n$th moment of a random variable about an arbitrary point, $a$ is $\mu_n = E[(X - a)^n]$, and if $a$ is equal to the expected value of $X$ then this is called the $n$th *central* moment. The first moment is the arithmetic mean of the random variable $X$, and the second moment along with the square of the first can be used to produce the variance: $VAR[X] = E[X^2] - E[X]^2$. While we are often interested only in the first two moments, the infinite moment property is very useful in assessing higher order moments in more complex settings. In general, it is straightforward to calculate the moment generating function and the cumulant generating function for exponential family forms. These are simply functions that provide any desired moment or cumulant (logged moments) with quick calculations.

Two important classes of probability density functions are not members of the exponential family. The student's $t$ and the uniform distribution cannot be put into the form of (2.1). In general, a probability function in which the parameterization is dependent on the bounds, such as the uniform distribution, are not members of the exponential family. Even if a probability function is not an exponential family member, it can sometimes qualify under particular circumstances. The Weibull probability density function (useful for modeling failure times), $f(y|\gamma, \beta) = (\gamma/\beta)y^{\gamma-1} \exp(-y^\gamma/\beta)$ for $x \geq 0, \gamma, \beta > 0$, is not an exponential family form since it cannot be rewritten in the required form (2.2). However, if $\gamma$ is known (or we are willing to assign an estimate), then the Weibull PDF reduces to an exponential family form.

Some widely used members of the exponential family that facilitate generalized linear models but are *not* discussed here include: beta, multinomial, curved normal, Dirichlet, Pareto, and inverse gamma. The theoretical focus of this monograph is intended to provide readers with an understanding necessary to successfully encounter these and other distributional forms.

## Derivation

Suppose we consider a one-parameter conditional probability density function or probability mass function for the random variable $Z$ of the form: $f(z|\zeta)$. This is read as "$f$ of $z$ given zeta." This function, or more specifically this family of PDFs or PMFs, is classified as an exponential family if it can be written in the form,

$$f(z|\zeta) = \exp[t(z)u(\zeta)]r(z)s(\zeta), \tag{2.1}$$

where: $r$ and $t$ are real-valued functions of $z$ that do not depend on $\zeta$, and $s$ and $u$ are real-valued functions of $\zeta$ that do not depend on $z$, and $r(z) > 0, s(\zeta) > 0 \; \forall z, \zeta$.

Furthermore, (2.1) can easily be rewritten as

$$f(z|\zeta) = \exp[\underbrace{t(z)u(\zeta)}_{\substack{\text{interaction} \\ \text{component}}} + \underbrace{\log(r(z)) + \log(s(\zeta))}_{\text{additive component}}]. \tag{2.2}$$

The second part of the right-hand side of the equation is labeled the "additive component" because the summed components are distinct and additive with regard to $z$ and $\zeta$. The first part of the right-hand side is labeled the "interaction component" because it is reminiscent of the interaction specification of two parameters in a standard linear model. In other words, it is the component that reflects the product-indistinguishable relationship between $z$ and $\zeta$. It should be noted that the interaction component must specify $t(z)u(\zeta)$ in a strictly multiplicative manner. So a term such as $-(1/\beta)y^\gamma$, as seen in the exponent of the Weibull PDF, disqualifies this PDF from the exponential family classification.

In addition, the exponential structure of (2.2) is preserved under random sampling such that the joint density function of independent, identically distributed (i.i.d.) $\mathbf{Z} = \{Z_1, Z_2, \dots, Z_n\}$ is

$$f(\mathbf{z}|\zeta) = \exp\left[u(\zeta)\sum_{i=1}^{n} t(z_i) + \sum_{i=1}^{n}\log(r(z_i)) + n\log(s(\zeta))\right]. \tag{2.3}$$

This means that the joint distribution of a systematic random sample of variates with exponential family marginal distributions is also an exponential family form. While the following chapters develop the theory of generalized linear models with (2.2) for simplicity, the joint density function, (2.3), is the more appropriate form since data are used. Fortunately there is no loss of generality since the joint density function is also an exponential family form. If it makes the exposition easier to follow, picture (2.2) with subscript $i$ as an index of the data: $f(z_i|\zeta) = \exp[t(z_i)u(\zeta) + \log(r(z_i)) + \log(s(\zeta))]$.

## Canonical Form

The canonical form is a handy simplification that greatly facilitates moment calculations as shown in Chapter 3. It is a one-to-one transformation (i.e., the inverse function of this function returns the same unique value) of terms of the probability function that reduces the complexity of the symbolism and reveals structure. It turns out to be much easier to work with an exponential family form when the format of the terms in the function says something directly about the behavior of the data.

If $t(z) = z$ in (2.2), then we say that this PDF or PMF is in its canonical form for the random variable $Z$. Otherwise we can make the simple transformation: $y = t(z)$ to force a canonical form. Similarly, if $u(\zeta) = \zeta$ in (2.2), then this PDF or PMF is in its canonical form for the parameter $\zeta$. Again, if not, we can force a canonical form by transforming: $\theta = u(\zeta)$, and call $\theta$ the canonical parameter.

In many cases it is not necessary to perform these transformations as the canonical form already exists or the transformed functions are tabulated for various exponential families of distributions. The final form after these transformations is the following general expression:

$$f(y|\theta) = \exp[y\theta - b(\theta) + c(y)]. \tag{2.4}$$

Note that the only term with both $y$ and $\theta$ is a multiplicative term. McCullagh and Nelder (1989, p. 30) call $b(\theta)$ the "cumulant function," but $b(\theta)$ is also often called a "normalizing constant" because it is the only nonfunction of the data and can therefore be manipulated to ensure that (2.4) sums or integrates to one. This is a minor point here as all of the commonly applied forms of (2.4) are well behaved in this respect. More importantly, $b(\theta)$ will play a key role in calculating the moments of the distribution. In addition, the form of $\theta$, the *canonical link* between the original form and the $\theta$ parameterized form, is also important. The canonical link is used to generalize the linear model by connecting the linear-additive component to the nonnormal outcome variable.

The form of (2.4) is not unique in that linear transformations can be applied to exchange values of $y$ and $\theta$ between the additive component and the interaction component. In general, however, common families of PDFs and PMFs are typically parameterized in a standard form which minimizes the number of interaction terms. Also, it will sometimes be helpful to use (2.4) expressed as a joint distribution of the data, particularly when working with the likelihood function (Chapter 3). This is just:

$$f(\mathbf{y}|\theta) = \exp\left[ \sum_{i=1}^{n} y_i\theta - nb(\theta) + \sum_{i=1}^{n} c(y_i) \right]. \tag{2.5}$$

The canonical form is used in each of the developed examples in this monograph. There is absolutely no information gained or lost by this treatment, rather the form of (2.5) is an equivalent form to (2.3) where certain structures such as $\theta$ and $b(\theta)$ are isolated for theoretical consideration. As will be shown, these terms are the key to generalizing the linear model.

**Multiparameter Models**

Up until now only single parameter forms have been presented. If generalized linear models were confined to single parameter density functions, they would be quite restrictive. Suppose now that there are $k$ parameters specified. A $k$-dimensional parameter vector, rather than just a scalar $\theta$, is now easily incorporated into the exponential family form of (2.4):

$$f(y|\boldsymbol{\theta}) = \exp\left[ \sum_{j=1}^{k} y\theta_j - b(\theta_j) + c(y) \right]. \tag{2.6}$$

Here the dimension of $\boldsymbol{\theta}$ can be arbitrarily large, but is often as small as 2, as in the normal ($\boldsymbol{\theta} = \{\mu, \sigma^2\}$) or the gamma ($\boldsymbol{\theta} = \{\alpha, \beta\}$).

In the following examples, several common probability functions are rewritten in exponential family form with the intermediate steps shown (for the most part). It is actually not strictly necessary to show the process since the number of PDFs and PMFs of interest is relatively small. However, there is great utility in seeing the steps both as an instructional exercise and as a starting point for other distributions of interest not covered herein. Also, in each case the $b(\theta)$ term is derived. The importance of doing this will be apparent in Chapter 3.

*Example 2.1: Poisson Distribution.* The Poisson distribution is often used to model counts such as the number of arrivals, deaths, or failures, in a given time period. The Poisson distribution assumes that for short time intervals, the probability of an arrival is fixed and proportional to the length of the interval. It is indexed by only one (necessarily positive) parameter which is both the mean and variance.

Given the random variable, $Y$, distributed Poisson with expected number of occurrences per interval $\mu$, we can rewrite the familiar Poisson PMF in the following manner:

$$f(y|\mu) = \frac{e^{-\mu}\mu^y}{y!} = \exp\left[\underbrace{y\log(\mu)}_{y\theta} - \underbrace{\mu}_{b(\theta)} \underbrace{-\log(y!)}_{c(y)}\right].$$

In this example, the three components from (2.4) are labeled by the underbraces. The interaction component, $y\log(\mu)$, clearly identifies $\theta = \log(\mu)$ as the canonical link. Also $b(\theta)$ is simply $\mu$. Therefore, the $b(\theta)$ term parameterized by $\theta$ (i.e., the canonical form) is obtained by taking the inverse of $\theta = \log(\mu)$ to solve for $\mu$. This produces:

$$\mu = \boxed{b(\theta) = \exp(\theta)}.$$

Obviously the Poisson distribution is a simple parametric form in this regard.

*Example 2.2: Binomial Distribution.* The binomial distribution summarizes the outcome of multiple binary outcome (Bernoulli) trials such as flipping a coin. This distribution is particularly useful for modeling counts of successes or failures given a number of independent trials such as votes received given an electorate, international wars given country-dyads in a region, or bankruptcies given company starts.

Suppose now that $Y$ is distributed binomial $(n, p)$ where $Y$ is the number of "successes" in a known number of $n$ trials given a probability of success $p$. We can rewrite the binomial PMF in exponential family form as[4]

$$f(y|n, p) = \binom{n}{y} p^y (1 - p)^{n-y}$$

$$= \exp\left[ \log\binom{n}{y} + y\log(p) + (n - y)\log(1 - p) \right]$$

$$= \exp\left[ \underbrace{y\log\left(\frac{p}{1-p}\right)}_{y\theta} - \underbrace{(-n\log(1 - p))}_{b(\theta)} + \underbrace{\log\binom{n}{y}}_{c(y)} \right].$$

From the first term in the exponent, we can see that the canonical link for the binomial distribution is $\theta = \log(p/(1 - p))$, so substituting the inverse of the canonical link function into $b(\theta)$ produces (with modest algebra):

$$b(\theta) = [-n\log(1 - p)]\Big|_{\theta=\log(p/(1-p))} = n\log(1 + \exp(\theta)).$$

So the expression for the $b(\theta)$ term in terms of the canonical parameter is:

$$\boxed{b(\theta) = n\log(1 + \exp(\theta))}.$$

In this example, $n$ was treated as a known quantity or simply ignored as a nuisance parameter. Suppose instead that $p$ was known and we developed the exponential family PMF with $n$ as the parameter of interest,

$$f(y|n, p) = \exp\left[ \log\binom{n}{y} + y\log(p) + (n - y)\log(1 - p) \right]$$

$$= \exp[\log(n!) - \log((n - y)!) - \log(y!) + \cdots]. \quad (2.7)$$

However, we cannot separate $n$ and $y$ in $\log((n - y)!)$ and they are not in product form, so this is not an exponential family PMF in this context.

*Example 2.3: Normal Distribution.* The normal distribution is without question the workhorse of social science data analysis. Given its simplicity in practice and well-understood theoretical foundations, this is not surprising. The linear model (OLS) is based on normal distribution theory and, as we shall see in Chapter 4, this comprises a very simple special case of the generalized linear model.

Often we need to explicitly treat nuisance parameters instead of ignoring them or assuming they are known as was done in the previous binomial example. The most important case of a two parameter exponential family is when the second parameter is a scale parameter. Suppose $\psi$ is such a scale parameter, then expression (2.4) is rewritten:

$$f(y|\theta) = \exp\left[\frac{y\theta - b(\theta)}{a(\psi)} + c(y, \psi)\right]. \qquad (2.8)$$

When a given PDF or PMF does not have a scale parameter then $a(\psi) = 1$, and (2.8) reduces to (2.4). In addition, (2.8) can be put into the more general form of (2.6) if we define $\boldsymbol{\theta} = \{\theta, a(\psi)^{-1}\}$ and rearrange. However, this form would no longer remind us of the important role the scale parameter plays.

The Gaussian normal distribution fits this class of exponential families. The subclass is called a location-scale family and has the attribute that it is fully specified by two parameters: a centering or location parameter, and a dispersion parameter. It can be rewritten,

$$
\begin{aligned}
f(y|\mu, \sigma^2) &= \frac{1}{\sqrt{2\pi\sigma^2}} \exp\left[-\frac{1}{2\sigma^2}(y - \mu)^2\right] \\
&= \exp\left[-\frac{1}{2}\log(2\pi\sigma^2) - \frac{1}{2\sigma^2}(y^2 - 2y\mu + \mu^2)\right] \\
&= \exp\left[\underbrace{\left(\underbrace{y\mu}_{y\theta} - \underbrace{\frac{\mu^2}{2}}_{b(\theta)}\right)/\underbrace{\sigma^2}_{a(\psi)}} + \underbrace{\frac{-1}{2}\left(\frac{y^2}{\sigma^2} + \log(2\pi\sigma^2)\right)}_{c(y,\psi)}\right].
\end{aligned}
$$

Note that the $\mu$ parameter (the mean) is already in canonical form $(\theta = \mu)$, so $b(\theta)$ is simply:

$$\boxed{b(\theta) = \frac{\theta^2}{2}}.$$

This treatment assumes that $\mu$ is the parameter of interest and $\sigma^2$ is the nuisance parameter, but we might want to look at the opposite situation. However, in this treatment, $\mu$ is not considered a scale parameter. Treating $\sigma^2$ as the variable of interest produces,

$$f(y|\mu, \sigma^2) = \exp\left[-\frac{1}{2}\log(2\pi\sigma^2) - \frac{1}{2\sigma^2}(y^2 - 2y\mu - \mu^2)\right]$$

$$= \exp\left[\underbrace{\frac{1}{\sigma^2}}_{\theta}\underbrace{\left(y\mu - \frac{1}{2}y^2\right)}_{z} + \underbrace{\frac{-1}{2}\left(\log(2\pi\sigma^2) - \frac{\mu^2}{\sigma^2}\right)}_{b(\theta)}\right].$$

Now the canonical link is $\theta = 1/\sigma^2$. So $\sigma^2 = \theta^{-1}$, and we can calculate the new $b(\theta)$:

$$b(\theta) = -\frac{1}{2}\left(\log(2\pi\sigma^2) - \frac{\mu^2}{\sigma^2}\right)$$

$$= -\frac{1}{2}\log(2\pi) + \frac{1}{2}\log(\theta) + \frac{1}{2}\mu^2\theta.$$

*Example 2.4: Gamma Distribution.* The gamma distribution is particularly useful for modeling terms that are required to be nonnegative such as variances. Furthermore, the gamma distribution has two important special cases: the $\chi^2$ distribution is gamma $(\rho/2, \frac{1}{2})$ for $\rho$ degrees of freedom, and the exponential distribution is gamma $(1, \beta)$, both of which arise quite often in applied settings.

Assume $Y$ is now distributed gamma indexed by two parameters: the shape parameter, and the inverse-scale parameter. The gamma distribution is most commonly written as

$$f(y|\alpha, \beta) = \frac{1}{\Gamma(\alpha)}\beta^\alpha y^{\alpha-1}e^{-\beta y}, \qquad y, \alpha, \beta > 0.$$

For our purposes, a more convenient form is produced by transforming: $\alpha = \delta, \beta = \delta/\mu$. The exponential family form of the gamma is

18

produced by

$$f(y|\mu,\delta) = \left(\frac{\delta}{\mu}\right)^{\delta} \frac{1}{\Gamma(\delta)} y^{\delta-1} \exp\left[\frac{-\delta y}{\mu}\right]$$

$$= \exp\left[\delta \log(\delta) - \delta \log(\mu) - \log(\Gamma(\delta)) + (\delta-1)\log(y) - \frac{\delta y}{\mu}\right]$$

$$= \exp\left[\left(-\frac{1}{\mu}y - \log(\mu)\right) \Big/ \frac{1}{\delta}\right.$$

$$\underbrace{\phantom{-\frac{1}{\mu}y}}_{\theta y} \underbrace{\phantom{-\log(\mu)}}_{b(\theta)} \underbrace{\phantom{\frac{1}{\delta}}}_{a(\psi)}$$

$$\left. + \underbrace{\delta \log(\delta) + (\delta-1)\log(y) - \log(\Gamma(\delta))}_{c(y,\psi)}\right].$$

From the first term in the last equation, the canonical link for the gamma family variable $\mu$, is $\theta = -1/\mu$. So $b(\theta) = \log(\mu) = \log(-1/\theta)$ with the restriction: $\theta < 0$. Therefore:

$$\boxed{b(\theta) = -\log(-\theta)}.$$

*Example 2.5: Negative Binomial Distribution.* The binomial distribution measures the number of successes in a given number of fixed trials, whereas the negative binomial distribution measures the number of failures before the $r$th success.[5] An important application of the negative binomial distribution is in survey research design. If the researcher knows the value of $p$ from previous surveys, then the negative binomial can provide the number of subjects to contact to get the desired number of responses for analysis.

If $Y$ is a distributed negative binomial with success probability $p$ and a goal of $r$ successes, then the PMF in exponential family form is produced by

$$f(y|r,p) = \binom{r+y-1}{y} p^r (1-p)^y$$

$$= \exp\left[\underbrace{y\log(1-p)}_{y\theta} + \underbrace{r\log(p)}_{b(\theta)} + \underbrace{\log\binom{r+y-1}{y}}_{c(y)}\right].$$

The canonical link is easily identified as $\theta = \log(1 - p)$. Substituting this into $b(\theta)$ and applying some algebra gives

$$\boxed{b(\theta) = r \log(1 - \exp(\theta))}.$$

We have now shown that some of the most useful and popular PMFs and PDFs can easily be represented in the exponential family form. The payoff for this effort is yet to come, but it can readily be seen that if $b(\theta)$ has particular theoretical significance then isolating it as we have in the $\theta$ parameterization is helpful. This is exactly the case as $b(\theta)$ is the engine for producing moments from the exponential family form through some basic likelihood theory. In addition, this chapter has a utility even for those sceptical of the generalized linear model framework. The reparameterization of commonly used PDFs and PMFs into the exponential family form highlights some well-known, but not necessarily intuitive relationships between parametric forms. For instance, virtually all introductory statistics texts explain that the normal distribution is the limiting form for the binomial distribution. Setting the first and second derivatives of the $b(\theta)$ function in these forms equal to each other gives the appropriate asymptotic reparameterization: $\mu = np$, $\sigma^2 = np(1 - p)$.

## 3. LIKELIHOOD THEORY AND THE MOMENTS

### Maximum Likelihood Estimation

To make inferences about the unknown parameters, we would like to develop the likelihood and score functions for (2.4). Maximizing the likelihood function with regard to coefficient values is without question the most frequently used estimation technique in applied statistics. Since asymptotic theory assures us that for sufficiently large samples the likelihood surface is unimodal in $k$ dimensions for exponential family forms (Fahrmeir & Kaufman, 1985; Jørgensen, 1983; Wedderburn, 1976), then this process is equivalent to finding the $k$-dimensional mode.

Our real interest lies in obtaining the posterior distribution of the unknown $k$-dimensional $\theta$ coefficient vector, given an observed matrix of data values: $f(\theta|X)$. This allows us to determine the "most likely" values of the $\theta$ vector using the $k$-dimensional mode (maximum likelihood inference, Fisher, 1925), or simply to probabilistically describe this distribution (as in Bayesian inference). This posterior is produced by the application of Bayes law,

$$f(\theta|X) = f(X|\theta)\frac{P(\theta)}{P(X)}, \qquad (3.1)$$

where $f(X|\theta)$ is the $n$-dimensional joint PDF or PMF of the data (*the probability of the sample* for a fixed $\theta$) under the assumption that the data are independent and identically distributed according to $f(X_i|\theta)$ $\forall i = 1, \ldots, n$, and $P(\theta), P(X)$ are the corresponding unconditional probabilities.

The Bayesian approach integrates out $P(X)$ (or ignores it using proportionality) and stipulates an assumed (prior) distribution on $\theta$, thus allowing fairly direct computation of $f(\theta|X)$ from (3.1). If we regard $f(X|\theta)$ as a function of $\theta$ for given observed data $X$ (we can consider the observed data as fixed, $P(X) = 1$, since it occurred), then $L(\theta|X) = f(X|\theta)$ is called a likelihood function (DeGroot, 1986, p. 339). The maximum likelihood principle states that an admissible $\theta$ that maximizes likelihood function probability (discrete case) or density (continuous case), relative to alternative values of $\theta$ provides the $\theta$ that is most "likely" to have generated the observed data: $X$, given the assumed parametric form. Restated, if $\hat{\theta}$ is the maximum likelihood estimator for the unknown parameter vector, then it is necessarily true that $L(\hat{\theta}|X) \geq L(\theta|X)$ $\forall \theta \in \Theta$, where $\Theta$ is the admissible range of $\theta$.

The likelihood function differs from the inverse probability, $f(\theta|X)$, in that it is necessarily a *relative* function since probabilistic uncertainty is a characteristic of the random variable $X$ not the unknown but fixed $\theta$. Barnett (1973, p. 131) clarifies this distinction: "Probability remains attached to $X$, not $\theta$; it simply reflects inferentially on $\theta$." Thus, maximum likelihood estimation substitutes the unbounded notion of likelihood for the bounded definition of probability (Barnett, 1973, p. 131; Casella & Berger, 1990, p. 266; Fisher, 1922, p. 327; King, 1989, p. 23). This is an important theoretical distinction, but of little significance in applied practice.

Typically, it is mathematically more convenient to work with the natural log of the likelihood function. This does not change any of the resulting parameter estimates because the likelihood function and the log likelihood function have identical modal points. Using (2.4), with the scale parameter added (as in the normal example) and returning to a single parameter of interest, $\theta$, case accompanied by a scale parameter, $a(\phi)$, the basic likelihood function is very simple:

$$
\begin{aligned}
l(\theta, \psi | \mathbf{y}) &= \log(f(\mathbf{y} | \theta, \psi)) \\
&= \log\left(\exp\left[\frac{\mathbf{y}\theta - b(\theta)}{a(\psi)} + c(\mathbf{y}, \psi)\right]\right) \\
&= \frac{\mathbf{y}\theta - b(\theta)}{a(\psi)} + c(\mathbf{y}, \psi).
\end{aligned} \tag{3.2}
$$

It is certainly not a coincidence that working with the natural log of the exponential family form simplifies our calculations. One of the reasons for casting all of the terms into the exponent is that at this stage the exponent becomes expendable and the terms are easy to work with.

The score function is the first derivative of the log likelihood function with respect to the parameters of interest. For the time being the scale parameter, $\psi$, is treated as a nuisance parameter. The resulting score function, denoted as $\dot{l}(\theta | \psi, \mathbf{y})$, is produced by

$$
\begin{aligned}
\dot{l}(\theta | \psi, \mathbf{y}) &= \frac{\partial}{\partial\theta} l(\theta | \psi, \mathbf{y}) \\
&= \frac{\partial}{\partial\theta}\left[\frac{\mathbf{y}\theta - b(\theta)}{a(\psi)} + c(\mathbf{y}, \psi)\right] \\
&= \frac{\mathbf{y} - \partial/\partial\theta\, b(\theta)}{a(\psi)}.
\end{aligned} \tag{3.3}
$$

Setting $\dot{l}(\theta | \psi, \mathbf{y})$ equal to zero and solving for the parameter of interest gives the maximum likelihood estimate, $\hat{\theta}$. This is now the most likely value of $\theta$ from the parameter space $\Theta$ treating the observed data as given: $\hat{\theta}$ maximizes the likelihood function at the observed values. The *Likelihood Principle* (Birnbaum, 1962) states that once the data are observed, and therefore treated as given, all of the available evidence for estimating $\hat{\theta}$ is contained in the likelihood function,

$l(\theta, \psi|\mathbf{y})$. This is a very handy data reduction tool because it tells us exactly what treatment of the data is important to us and allows us to ignore an infinite number of alternates.

Suppose we use the notation for the exponential family form expressed as the joint probability function of the observed independent, identically distributed (i.i.d) data (2.5): $f(\mathbf{y}|\theta) = \exp[\Sigma_{i=1}^{n} y_i \theta - nb(\theta) + \Sigma_{i=1}^{n} c(y_i)]$. Setting the score function from this joint PDF or PMF equal to zero and rearranging gives the likelihood equation,

$$\sum t(y_i) = n\frac{\partial}{\partial\theta} \log(b(\theta)), \qquad (3.4)$$

where $\Sigma t(y_i)$ is the remaining function of the data, depending on the form of the PDF or PMF. The underlying theory is remarkably strong. Solving (3.4) for the unknown coefficient produces an estimator that is unique (a unimodal posterior distribution), consistent (converges in probability), and asymptotically efficient (the variance of the estimator achieves the lowest possible value as the sample size becomes adequately large: the Cramér–Rao lower bound). This combined with the central limit theorem gives the asymptotic normal form for the estimator: $\sqrt{n}(\hat{\theta} - \theta)\xrightarrow{\mathscr{D}} n(0, \Sigma_\theta)$. Furthermore, $\Sigma t(y_i)$ is a sufficient statistic for $\theta$, meaning that all of the relevant information about $\theta$ in the data is contained in $\Sigma t(y_i)$. For example, the normal log likelihood expressed as a joint exponential family form as in (2.5) is $l(\theta, \psi|\mathbf{y}) = (\mu\Sigma y_i - n\mu^2/2)/\sigma^2 - (1/2\sigma^2)\Sigma y_i^2 - (n/2) \log(2\pi\sigma^2)$. So, $t(\mathbf{y}) = \Sigma y_i$, $\partial/\partial\theta(n\mu^2/2) = n\mu$ and equating gives the maximum likelihood estimate of $\mu$ to be the sample average which we know from basic texts: $(1/n)\Sigma y_i$.

### Calculating the Mean of the Exponential Family

An important quantity to calculate is the mean of the PDF or PMF in the context of (2.4). The generalization of the linear model is done by connecting the linear predictor, $\boldsymbol{\theta} = \mathbf{X}\boldsymbol{\beta}$, from a standard linear models analysis of the explanatory variables to the nonnormal outcome variable through its mean function. Therefore, the expected value (first moment) plays a key theoretical role in the development of generalized linear models. The expected value calculation of (2.4) with respect to the data $(Y)$ is

$$E_Y\left[\frac{y - \partial/\partial\theta b(\theta)}{a(\psi)}\right] = 0,$$

$$\int_Y \frac{y - \partial/\partial\theta b(\theta)}{a(\psi)} f(y)\, d(y) = 0,$$

$$\int_Y yf(y)\, dy - \int_Y \frac{\partial b(\theta)}{\partial\theta} f(y)\, dy = 0, \qquad (3.5)$$

$$\underbrace{\int_Y yf(y)\, dy}_{E[Y]} - \frac{\partial b(\theta)}{\partial\theta} \underbrace{\int_Y f(y)\, dy}_{1} = 0.$$

The last step requires general regularity conditions[6] with regard to the bounds of integration and all exponential family distributions meet this requirement (Casella & Berger, 1990). From this derivation,[7] we get the wonderfully useful result that

$$\boxed{E[Y] = \tfrac{\partial}{\partial\theta} b(\theta)}.$$

So all that is required from (2.4) to get the mean of a particular exponential family of distributions, a quantity I will call $\mu$ for uniformity across examples, is $b(\theta)$. This is an illustration of the value of expressing exponential family distributions in canonical form, since the first derivative of $b(\theta)$ immediately produces the first moment.

*Example 3.1: Mean for the Poisson Probability Mass Functions.* The procedure for obtaining the expected value (mean) is just to perform the differentiation of $b(\theta)$ with regard to $\theta$ and then substitute in the canonical link and solve. Generally this is a very simple process.

Recall that for the Poisson distribution: the normalizing constant is $b(\theta) = \exp(\theta)$, and the canonical link function is $\theta = \log(\mu)$. So

$$\frac{\partial}{\partial\theta} b(\theta) = \frac{\partial}{\partial\theta} \exp(\theta) = \exp(\theta)\big|_{\theta=\log(\mu)} = \mu.$$

Of course the result that

$$\boxed{E[Y] = \mu}$$

for a Poisson distributed random variable is exactly what we would expect.

*Example 3.2: Mean for the Binomial Probability Mass Function.* For the binomial distribution, $b(\theta) = n \log(1 + \exp(\theta))$, and $\theta = \log(p/(1 - p))$. Therefore, from the following we get the mean function,

$$\frac{\partial}{\partial \theta} b(\theta) = \frac{\partial}{\partial \theta}(n \log(1 + \exp(\theta)))$$

$$= n(1 + \exp(\theta))^{-1} \exp(\theta)\big|_{\theta = \log(p/(1-p))}$$

$$= n\left(1 + \exp\left(\log\left(\frac{p}{1 - p}\right)\right)\right)^{-1} \exp\left(\log\left(\frac{p}{p - 1}\right)\right)$$

$$= n(1 - p)\left(\frac{p}{p - 1}\right),$$

where some algebra is required in addition to taking the derivative. Once again

$$\boxed{E[Y] = np}$$

is the expected result from standard moments analysis.

*Example 3.3: Mean for the Normal Probability Density Function.* The normal form of the exponential family has $b(\theta) = \theta^2/2$, and simply $\theta = \mu$. Therefore,

$$\frac{\partial}{\partial \theta} b(\theta) = \frac{\partial}{\partial \theta}\left(\frac{\theta^2}{2}\right) = \theta\big|_{\theta = \mu}. \tag{3.6}$$

This is the most straightforward and important case:

$$\boxed{E[Y] = \mu}.$$

*Example 3.4: Mean for the Gamma Probability Density Function.* Recall that for the gamma exponential family form, $\theta = -1/\mu$ and $b(\theta) = -\log(-\theta)$. This produces:

$$\frac{\partial}{\partial \theta} b(\theta) = \frac{\partial}{\partial \theta}(-\log(-\theta)) = -\frac{1}{\theta}\big|_{\theta = -1/\mu} = \mu.$$

For the gamma distribution, we found that

$$\boxed{E[Y] = \mu}.$$

This is equivalent to $E[Y] = \alpha/\beta$ when the gamma PDF is expressed in the familiar form:

$$f(y|\alpha, \beta) = \frac{1}{\Gamma(\alpha)}\beta^\alpha y^{\alpha-1}e^{-\beta y}, \qquad (\mu = \alpha\beta, \delta = \alpha).$$

*Example 3.5: Mean for the Negative Binomial Probability Mass Function.* For the negative binomial distribution, $b(\theta) = r\log(1 - \exp(\theta))$, and $\theta = \log(1 - p)$. The mean is obtained by

$$\begin{aligned}
\frac{\partial}{\partial\theta}b(\theta) &= \frac{\partial}{\partial\theta}r\log(1 - \exp(\theta)) \\
&= r(1 - \exp(\theta))^{-1}\exp(\theta)\big|_{\theta=\log(1-p)} \\
&= r\frac{1 - p}{1 - (1 - p)}.
\end{aligned}$$

So for the negative binomial we get the mean function

$$\boxed{E[Y] = r\frac{1-p}{p}}.$$

While this may seem like an inordinate amount of effort to specify mean functions for commonly used distributions, the value lies in further understanding the unified approach that results from expressing probability functions in exponential family form. The mean function is pivotal to the working of generalized linear models because, as we see in Chapter 4, the link function connects linear predictor to the mean of the exponential family form.

### Calculating the Variance of the Exponential Family

Just as we have derived the first moment in the previous text, we can obtain the variance from the second moment. Since $E[Y]=\partial/\partial\theta b(\theta)$ and $\dot{l}(\hat{\theta}, \psi|y) = 0$, then the variance calculations for the exponential family form are greatly simplified. First we obtain the variance and derivative of the score function and then apply a well-known mathematical statistics relationship.

The variance of the score function is

$$\text{VAR}[\dot{l}(\theta,\psi|y)] = E\left[\left(\dot{l}(\theta,\psi|y) - E[\dot{l}(\theta,\psi|y)]\right)^2\right] = E\left[\left(\dot{l}(\theta,\psi|y) - 0\right)^2\right]$$

$$= E\left[\left(\frac{y - \partial/\partial\theta b(\theta)}{a(\psi)}\right)^2\right] = E\left[\frac{(y - \partial/\partial\theta b(\theta))^2}{a^2(\psi)}\right]$$

$$= E\left[\frac{(y - E[Y])^2}{a^2(\psi)}\right]$$

$$= \frac{1}{a^2(\psi)} \text{VAR}[Y]. \tag{3.7}$$

The derivative of the score function with respect to $\theta$ is

$$\frac{\partial}{\partial\theta}\dot{l}(\theta,\psi|y) = \frac{\partial}{\partial\theta}\left(\frac{y - \partial/\partial\theta b(\theta)}{a(\psi)}\right) = -\frac{1}{a(\psi)}\frac{\partial^2}{\partial\theta^2}b(\theta). \tag{3.8}$$

The utility of deriving (3.7) and (3.8) comes from the relation: $E[(\dot{l}(\theta,\psi|y))^2] = E(-\partial/\partial\theta\dot{l}(\theta,\psi|y))$ for exponential families (Casella & Berger, 1990, p. 312). This means that we can equate (3.7) and (3.8) to solve for VAR[Y],

$$\frac{1}{a^2(\psi)}\text{VAR}[Y] = \frac{1}{a(\psi)}\frac{\partial^2}{\partial\theta^2}b(\theta),$$

$$\text{VAR}[Y] = a(\psi)\frac{\partial^2}{\partial\theta^2}b(\theta). \tag{3.9}$$

We now have expressions for the mean and variance of $Y$ expressed in the terms of the exponential family format (2.4) with the $a(\psi)$ term included.

*Example 3.6: Variance for the Poisson Probability Mass Function.*

$$\text{VAR}[Y] = a(\psi)\frac{\partial^2}{\partial\theta^2}b(\theta) = 1\frac{\partial^2}{\partial\theta^2}\exp(\theta)\big|_{\theta=\log(\mu)} = \exp(\log(\mu)) = \mu.$$

Once again

$$\boxed{\text{VAR}[Y] = \mu}$$

is the expected result.

*Example 3.7: Variance for the Binomial Probability Mass Function.*

$$\text{VAR}[Y] = a(\psi)\frac{\partial^2}{\partial\theta^2}b(\theta)$$

$$= 1\frac{\partial^2}{\partial\theta^2}(n\,\log(1+\exp(\theta)))$$

$$= \frac{\partial}{\partial\theta}(n(1+\exp(\theta))^{-1}\exp(\theta))$$

$$= n\,\exp(\theta)[(1+\exp(\theta))^{-1}$$

$$\qquad - (1+\exp(\theta))^{-2}\,\exp(\theta)]\big|_{\theta=\log(p/(1-p))}$$

$$= n\Big(\frac{p}{1-p}\Big)\Big[\Big(1+\frac{p}{1-p}\Big)^{-1} - \Big(1+\frac{p}{1-p}\Big)^{-2}\frac{p}{1-p}\Big]$$

$$= np(1-p).$$

$$\boxed{\text{VAR}[Y] = np(1-p)}$$

is the familiar form for the variance of the binomial distribution.

*Example 3.8: Variance for the Normal Probability Density Function.*

$$\text{VAR}[Y] = a(\psi)\frac{\partial^2}{\partial\theta^2}b(\theta) = \sigma^2\frac{\partial^2}{\partial\theta^2}\Big(\frac{\theta^2}{2}\Big) = \sigma^2\frac{\partial}{\partial\theta}\theta, \qquad (3.10)$$

$$\boxed{\text{VAR}[Y] = \sigma^2}$$

is the obvious result.

*Example 3.9: Variance for the Gamma Probability Density Function.*

$$\text{VAR}[Y] = a(\psi)\frac{\partial^2}{\partial\theta^2}b(\theta) = \frac{1}{\delta}\frac{\partial^2}{\partial\theta^2}(-\log(-\theta)) = \frac{1}{\delta}\frac{\partial}{\partial\theta}\Big(-\frac{1}{-\theta}(-1)\Big)$$

$$= -\frac{1}{\delta}((-1)\theta^{-2})\big|_{\theta=-1/\mu} = \frac{1}{\delta}\mu^2. \qquad (3.11)$$

This result,

$$\boxed{\text{VAR}[Y] = \tfrac{1}{\delta}\mu^2},$$

is equivalent to $\alpha/\beta^2$ in the other familiar notation for the gamma PDF.

*Example 3.10: Variance for the Negative Binomial Probability Mass Function.*

$$\text{VAR}[Y] = a(\psi)\frac{\partial^2}{\partial\theta^2}b(\theta)$$

$$= 1\frac{\partial}{\partial\theta}r(1-\exp(\theta))^{-1}\exp(\theta)$$

$$= r\exp(\theta)\left[(1-\exp(\theta))^{-2}\exp(\theta)+(1-\exp(\theta))^{-1}\right]\Big|_{\theta=\log(1-p)}$$

$$= r(1-p)\left[(1-(1-p))^{-2}(1-p)+(1-(1-p))^{-1}\right]$$

$$= \frac{r(1-p)}{p^2}.$$

Also,

$$\boxed{\text{VAR}[Y] = r(1-p)/p^2}$$

is exactly what we expected.

## The Variance Function

It is common to define a variance *function* for a given exponential family expression in which the $\theta$ notation is preserved for compatibility with the $b(\theta)$ form. The variance function is used in generalized linear models to indicate the dependence of the variance of $Y$ on location and scale parameters. It is also important in developing useful residuals analysis as discussed in Chapter 6. The variance function is simply defined as: $\tau^2 = \partial^2/\partial\theta^2 b(\theta)$, meaning that $\text{VAR}[Y] = a(\psi)\tau^2$ indexed by $\theta$. Note that the dependence on $b(\theta)$ explicitly states that the variance function is conditional on the mean function, whereas there was no such stipulation with the $a(\psi)$ form.

TABLE 3.1
Normalizing Constants and Variance Functions

| Distribution | $b(\theta)$ | $\tau^2 = \frac{\partial^2}{\partial\theta^2}b(\theta)$ |
|---|---|---|
| Poisson | $\exp(\theta)$ | $\exp(\theta)$ |
| Binomial | $n\log(1+\exp(\theta))$ | $n\exp(\theta)(1+\exp(\theta))^{-2}$ |
| Normal | $\frac{\theta^2}{2}$ | 1 |
| Gamma | $-\log(-\theta)$ | $\frac{1}{\theta^2}$ |
| Negative binomial | $r\log(1-\exp(\theta))$ | $r\exp(\theta)(1-\exp(\theta))^{-2}$ |

The variance of $Y$ can also be expressed with prior weighting, usually coming from point estimation theory: $\text{VAR}[Y] = (\Psi/w)\tau^2$ where $\Psi$ is a dispersion parameter and $w$ is a prior weight. For example, a mean from a sample of size $n$, and a population with known variance $\sigma^2$, is

$$\text{VAR}[\bar{X}] = \frac{\Psi\tau^2}{w} = \frac{\sigma^2}{n}.$$

It is convention to leave the variance function in terms of the canonical parameter, $\theta$, rather than return it to the parameterization in the original probability function as was done for the variance of $Y$. Table 3.1 summarizes the variance functions for the distributions studied.

## 4. LINEAR STRUCTURE AND THE LINK FUNCTION

This is the most important chapter of the monograph. It describes the theory by which the standard linear model is generalized to accommodate nonnormal outcome variables such as discrete choices, counts, survival periods, truncated varieties, and more. The basic philosophy is to employ a function of the mean vector to link the normal theory environment with Gauss–Markov assumptions, to another environment that encompasses a wide class of outcome variables.

The first part of this monograph explored the exponential family and showed how seemingly distinct probability functions had an underlying theoretical similarity. That similarity is exploited in this chapter by showing how the $\theta$ specification and the $b(\theta)$ function lead to logical link functions under general conditions.

## The Generalization

Consider the standard linear model meeting the Gauss–Markov conditions. This can be expressed as

$$\underset{(n \times 1)}{\mathbf{V}} = \underset{(n \times k)(k \times 1)}{\mathbf{X}\boldsymbol{\beta}} + \underset{(n \times 1)}{\boldsymbol{\epsilon}} , \qquad (4.1)$$

$$\underset{(n \times 1)}{E[\mathbf{V}]} = \underset{(n \times 1)}{\boldsymbol{\theta}} = \underset{(n \times k)(k \times 1)}{\mathbf{X}\boldsymbol{\beta}} . \qquad (4.2)$$

The right-hand sides of the two equations are very familiar: $\mathbf{X}$ is the design or model matrix of observed data values, $\boldsymbol{\beta}$ is the vector of unknown coefficients to be estimated, $\mathbf{X}\boldsymbol{\beta}$ is called the "linear structure vector," and $\boldsymbol{\epsilon}$ are the independent normally distributed error terms with constant variance: the random component. On the left-hand side of (4.2), $E[\mathbf{V}] = \boldsymbol{\theta}$ is the vector of means: the systematic component. The variable, $\mathbf{V}$, is distributed i.i.d. normal with mean $\boldsymbol{\theta}$, and constant variance $\sigma^2$. So far this is exactly the linear model described in basic statistics texts.

Now suppose we generalize slightly this well-known form with a new "linear predictor" based on the mean of the outcome variable,

$$\underset{(n \times 1)}{g(\boldsymbol{\mu})} = \underset{(n \times 1)}{\boldsymbol{\theta}} = \underset{(n \times k)\,(k \times 1)}{\mathbf{X}\boldsymbol{\beta}} ,$$

where $g(\ )$ is an invertible, *smooth* function of the mean vector $\boldsymbol{\mu}$ (i.e., no discontinuities). At this point we drop the $\mathbf{V}$ vector of normal variates completely since it is an artificial construct; these realizations never actually existed. The $\mathbf{V}$ vector is only useful in setting up the right-hand side of (4.1) and (4.2).

Information from the explanatory variables is now expressed only through the link from the linear structure, $\mathbf{X}\boldsymbol{\beta}$, to the linear predictor, $\boldsymbol{\theta} = g(\boldsymbol{\mu})$, controlled by the form of the link function, $g(\ )$. This link function connects the linear predictor to the *mean* of the outcome variable not directly to the expression of the outcome variable itself (as in the linear model), so the outcome variable can now take on a variety of nonnormal forms. By this manner, the generalized linear model extends the standard linear model to accommodate nonnormal response functions with transformations to linearity.

The generalization of the linear model now has three components derived from the previous expressions.

I. *Stochastic component*: **Y** is the random or stochastic component which remains distributed i.i.d. according to a specific exponential family distribution such as those in Chapter 2, with mean **μ**. This component is sometimes also called the "error structure," or "response distribution."

II. *Systematic component*: **θ** = **Xβ** is the systematic component producing the linear predictor. So the explanatory variables, **X**, affect the observed outcome variable, **Y**, *only* through the functional form of the $g(\ )$ function.

III. *Link function*: the stochastic component and the systematic component are linked by a function of **θ** which is *exactly the canonical link function* developed in Chapter 2 and summarized in Table 4.1. The link function connects the stochastic component which describes some response variable from a wide variety of forms to all of the standard normal theory supporting the systematic component through the mean function,

$$g(\mathbf{\mu}) = \mathbf{\theta} = \mathbf{X}\mathbf{\beta},$$

$$g^{-1}(g(\mathbf{\mu})) = g^{-1}(\mathbf{\theta}) = g^{-1}(\mathbf{X}\mathbf{\beta}) = \mathbf{\mu} = E[\mathbf{Y}].$$

So the inverse of the link function ensures that **Xβ̂**, where we insert **β̂** the estimated coefficient vector, maintains the Gauss–Markov assumptions for linear models and all of the standard theory applies even though the outcome variable takes on a variety of nonnormal forms.

TABLE 4.1
Natural Link Function Summary for Example Distributions

| Distribution | | Canonical Link: $\theta = g(\mu)$ | Inverse Link: $\mu = g^{-1}(\theta)$ |
|---|---|---|---|
| Poisson | | $\log(\mu)$ | $\exp(\theta)$ |
| Binomial | *logit link:* | $\log\left(\dfrac{\mu}{1-\mu}\right)$ | $\dfrac{\exp(\theta)}{1+\exp(\theta)}$ |
| | *probit link:* | $\Phi^{-1}(\mu)$ | $\Phi(\theta)$ |
| | *cloglog link:* | $\log(-\log(1-\mu))$ | $1-\exp(-\exp(\theta))$ |
| Normal | | $\mu$ | $\theta$ |
| Gamma | | $-\dfrac{1}{\mu}$ | $-\dfrac{1}{\theta}$ |
| Negative binomial | | $\log(1-\mu)$ | $1-\exp(\theta)$ |

We can think of $g(\mathbf{\mu})$ as "tricking" the linear model into thinking that it is still acting upon normally distributed outcome variables.

The link function connects the linear predictor, the systematic component ($\mathbf{\theta}$), to the expected value of the specified exponential family form ($\mathbf{\mu}$). This statement is much more powerful than it initially appears. The outcome variable described by the exponential family form is affected by the explanatory variables strictly through the link function applied to systematic component, $g^{-1}(\mathbf{X\beta})$, and nothing else. This data reduction is accomplished because $g^{-1}(\mathbf{X\beta})$ is a sufficient statistic for $\mathbf{\mu}$, given the assumed parametric form (PMF or PDF) and a correctly specified link function.

Actually, although it is traditional to describe the generalized linear model by these three components, there are really four. The residuals comprise the fourth component and are critical determinants of model quality, as shown in Chapter 6.

The payoff to notating and understanding distributions in exponential family form is that the canonical link function is simply the $\theta = u(\zeta)$ component from the interaction component in (2.2) expressed in canonical form. In other words, once the exponential family form is expressed, the link function is immediately identified. For example, since the exponential family form for the negative binomial PMF is

$$f(y|r, p) = \exp\left[ y\log(1 - p) + \log(p) + \log\left( \begin{matrix} r + y - 1 \\ y \end{matrix} \right) \right],$$

then the canonical link function is $\theta = \log(1 - p)$. Even more simply, in standard linear models the link function is the identity function: $\theta = \mu$. This states that the canonical parameter equals the systematic component, so the linear predictor is just the expected value.

### Distributions

Table 4.1 summarizes the link functions for the distributions included as running examples. Note that $g(\ )$ and $g^{-1}(\ )$ are both included.

In Table 4.1 there are three expressions for the canonical link for the binomial PMF. The first link function, *logit*, is the one that naturally occurs from the exponential family form expression for the canonical term (Example 2.2). The *probit* link function (based on the cumulative standard normal distribution, denoted Φ), and the *cloglog* link function are close but not exact approximations of the same mathematical form, and are practical conveniences rather than theoretically derived expressions. The differences are really apparent only in the tails of these distributions (especially with the cloglog). In general, with social science data any of these link functions can be used and will provide identical substantive conclusions.

*Example 4.1: Poisson Generalized Linear Model of Capital Punishment Data.* Consider an example in which the outcome variable is the number of times that capital punishment is implemented on a state level in the United States for the year 1997. Included in the data are explanatory variables for: median per capita income in dollars, the percent of the population classified as living in poverty, the percent of Black citizens in the population, the rate of violent crimes per 100,000 residents for the year before (1996), a dummy variable to indicate whether the state is in the South, and the proportion of the population with a college degree of some kind.[8] In 1997, executions were carried out in 17 states with a national total of 74. The original data for this problem are provided in Table 4.2 and constitute the **X** matrix in the earlier discussion (except that the **X** matrix necessarily contains a leading vector of ones for the constant instead of the outcome variable in the first column).

The model is developed from the Poisson link function in Table 4.1, $\theta = \log(\mu)$, with the objective of finding the best $\beta$ vector in

$$\underbrace{g^{-1}(\theta)}_{17 \times 1} = g^{-1}(\mathbf{X}\boldsymbol{\beta})$$

$$= \exp[\mathbf{X}\boldsymbol{\beta}]$$

$$= \exp[\mathbf{1}\beta_0 + \text{INC}\beta_1 + \text{POV}\beta_2 + \text{BLK}\beta_3 + \text{CRI}\beta_4$$

$$+ \text{SOU}\beta_5 + \text{DEG}\beta_6]$$

$$= E[\mathbf{Y}] = E[\text{EXE}].$$

The systematic component here is $\mathbf{X}\boldsymbol{\beta}$, the stochastic component is $\mathbf{Y} = \text{EXE}$, and the link function is $\theta = \log(\mu)$. The goal is to estimate the coefficient vector: $\boldsymbol{\beta} = \{\beta_0, \beta_1, \beta_2, \beta_3, \beta_4, \beta_5, \beta_6\}$ in the

TABLE 4.2
Capital Punishment in the United States—1997

| State | Executions | Median Income | Percent Poverty | Percent Black | Violent Crime/100 K | South | Proportion w/Degrees |
|---|---|---|---|---|---|---|---|
| Texas | 37 | 34,453 | 16.7 | 12.2 | 644 | 1 | 0.16 |
| Virginia | 9 | 41,534 | 12.5 | 20.0 | 351 | 1 | 0.27 |
| Missouri | 6 | 35,802 | 10.6 | 11.2 | 591 | 0 | 0.21 |
| Arkansas | 4 | 26,954 | 18.4 | 16.1 | 524 | 1 | 0.16 |
| Alabama | 3 | 31,468 | 14.8 | 25.9 | 565 | 1 | 0.19 |
| Arizona | 2 | 32,552 | 18.8 | 3.5 | 632 | 0 | 0.25 |
| Illinois | 2 | 40,873 | 11.6 | 15.3 | 886 | 0 | 0.25 |
| South Carolina | 2 | 34,861 | 13.1 | 30.1 | 997 | 1 | 0.21 |
| Colorado | 1 | 42,562 | 9.4 | 4.3 | 405 | 0 | 0.31 |
| Florida | 1 | 31,900 | 14.3 | 15.4 | 1051 | 1 | 0.24 |
| Indiana | 1 | 37,421 | 8.2 | 8.2 | 537 | 0 | 0.19 |
| Kentucky | 1 | 33,305 | 16.4 | 7.2 | 321 | 0 | 0.16 |
| Louisiana | 1 | 32,108 | 18.4 | 32.1 | 929 | 1 | 0.18 |
| Maryland | 1 | 45,844 | 9.3 | 27.4 | 931 | 0 | 0.29 |
| Nebraska | 1 | 34,743 | 10.0 | 4.0 | 435 | 0 | 0.24 |
| Oklahoma | 1 | 29,709 | 15.2 | 7.7 | 597 | 0 | 0.21 |
| Oregon | 1 | 36,777 | 11.7 | 1.8 | 463 | 0 | 0.25 |
| | EXE | INC | POV | BLK | CRI | SOU | DEG |

Source: U.S. Census Bureau, U.S. Department of Justice.

previous context. From this notation, it is clear that the rate of executions is affected by the explanatory variables only through the link function. It should also be noted that the quality of the model is still partly a function of appropriate variable inclusion, casewise independence, and measurement quality *exactly as in the standard linear model*. In this generalized linear model, we have the additional assumption that $\theta = \log(\mu)$ is the appropriate link function.

*Example 4.2: Gamma Generalized Linear Model of Electoral Politics in Scotland.* On September 11, 1997, Scottish voters overwhelmingly (74.3%) approved the establishment of the first Scottish national parliament in nearly 300 years. On the same ballot, the voters gave strong support (63.5%) to granting this parliament taxation powers. This vote represents a watershed event in the modern history of Scotland which was a free and independent country until 1707. Whether this event is simply an incremental part of the current Labor government's decentralization program or a genuine step toward renewed Scottish independence within Europe remains an open question.

The popular press in the United Kingdom and elsewhere emphasized Scottish pride and nationalism as driving factors in the voters' minds. The question addressed here is whether or not social and economic factors were important as perhaps more rational determinants of the vote. The data are aggregated to 32 *unitary authorities* (also called council districts). These are the official local divisions in Scotland since 1996, before which there were 12 administrative regions. Despite the greater journalistic attention paid to the first vote establishing the Scottish parliament, it can be argued that granting taxation powers to a new legislature is more consequential. The outcome variable analyzed here is therefore the protaxation granting vote percentage measured at the council district level.

The data set, collected from U.K. government sources, includes 40 potential explanatory variables from which 6 are selected for this model (all 40 are available to readers in the data set provided at my website). Because the other local taxing body is the council, a variable for the amount of council tax is included, measured in £ Sterling as of April, 1997 per two adults before miscellaneous adjustments. The data include several variables concerning employment and unemployment benefits. The variable selected here is the female percentage of total claims for unemployment benefits as of January, 1998. Due to the complexities of measuring actual unemployment rates from nationally collected statistics on those who apply for benefits, female applicants appear to be a better indication of underlying unemployment activity in Scotland: they are more likely to apply when unemployed and less likely to participate in unrecorded economic activities. As a way of measuring regional variation in population aging, the standardized mortality rate (United Kingdom equals 100) is included. Interestingly, this measure is higher than the U.K. benchmark in 30 of the 32 Scottish council districts. To include general labor force activity, a variable is specified indicating the percent of economically active individuals relative to the population of working age. Finally, as a way to look at family size and perhaps commitment to community building (and therefore an implied tolerance for greater taxation), the percentage of children aged 5 to 15 is included.

As a percentage (actually converted to a proportion here simply to make the scale of the coefficient estimates more readable) the outcome variable is bounded by zero and 100. It is regrettably common to see researchers apply the standard linear model in this setting and then obtain estimates from ordinary least squares estimation. This is a flawed practice, but in varying degrees. If the data are centered in the middle of the interval and no censoring is involved at the bounds, then the results, while theoretically unjustified, are likely to be quite reasonable. However, if the data are concentrated at either end of the interval or there is some amount of censoring at the bounds, then serious errors of estimation can occur.[9] An appropriate model, provided that there is no censoring at the upper bound, is a generalized linear model with the gamma link function. This model is often used to model variance since the outcome variable is defined over the sample space $[0, +\infty]$. Because vote percentages over 100 are not defined and do not exist, then this is a good choice of model for this example.

The model for these data using the gamma link function is produced by

$$\underbrace{g^{-1}(\boldsymbol{\theta})}_{32 \times 1} = g^{-1}(\mathbf{X}\boldsymbol{\beta})$$

$$= -\frac{1}{\mathbf{X}\boldsymbol{\beta}}$$

$$= -[1\beta_0 + \mathrm{COU}\beta_1 + \mathrm{UNM}\beta_2 + \mathrm{MOR}\beta_3 + \mathrm{ACT}\beta_4 + \mathrm{AGE}\beta_5]^{-1}$$

$$= E[\mathbf{Y}] = E[\mathbf{YES}].$$

TABLE 4.3
Taxation Powers Vote for the Scottish Parliament—1997

| | Proportion Voting Yes | Council Tax | % Female Unemployment | Standardized Mortality | % Active Economically | % Aged 5–15 |
|---|---|---|---|---|---|---|
| Aberdeen City | 0.603 | 712 | 21.0 | 105 | 82.4 | 12.3 |
| Aberdeenshire | 0.523 | 643 | 26.5 | 97 | 80.2 | 15.3 |
| Angus | 0.534 | 679 | 28.3 | 113 | 86.3 | 13.9 |
| Argyil & Bute | 0.570 | 801 | 27.1 | 109 | 80.4 | 13.6 |
| Clackmannanshire | 0.687 | 753 | 22.0 | 115 | 64.7 | 14.6 |
| Dumfries & Galloway | 0.488 | 714 | 24.3 | 107 | 79.0 | 13.8 |
| Dundee City | 0.655 | 920 | 21.2 | 118 | 72.2 | 13.3 |
| East Ayrshire | 0.705 | 779 | 20.5 | 114 | 75.2 | 14.5 |
| East Dunbartonshire | 0.591 | 771 | 23.2 | 102 | 81.1 | 14.2 |
| East Lothian | 0.627 | 724 | 20.5 | 112 | 80.3 | 13.7 |
| East Renfrewshire | 0.516 | 682 | 23.8 | 96 | 83.0 | 14.6 |
| Edinburgh City | 0.620 | 837 | 22.1 | 111 | 74.5 | 11.6 |
| Western Isles | 0.684 | 599 | 19.9 | 117 | 83.8 | 15.1 |
| Falkirk | 0.692 | 680 | 21.5 | 121 | 77.6 | 13.7 |
| Fife | 0.647 | 747 | 22.5 | 109 | 77.9 | 14.4 |
| Glasgow City | 0.750 | 982 | 19.4 | 137 | 65.3 | 13.3 |
| Highland | 0.621 | 719 | 25.9 | 109 | 80.9 | 14.9 |

TABLE 4.3
Continued

| | Proportion Voting Yes | Council Tax | % Female Unemployment | Standardized Mortality | % Active Economically | % Aged 5–15 |
|---|---|---|---|---|---|---|
| Inverclyde | 0.672 | 831 | 18.5 | 138 | 80.2 | 14.6 |
| Midlothian | 0.677 | 858 | 19.4 | 119 | 84.8 | 14.3 |
| Moray | 0.527 | 652 | 27.2 | 108 | 86.4 | 14.6 |
| North Ayrshire | 0.657 | 718 | 23.7 | 115 | 73.5 | 15.0 |
| North Lanarkshir | 0.722 | 787 | 20.8 | 126 | 74.7 | 14.9 |
| Orkney Islands | 0.474 | 515 | 26.8 | 106 | 87.8 | 15.3 |
| Perth and Kinross | 0.513 | 732 | 23.0 | 103 | 86.6 | 13.8 |
| Renfrewshire | 0.636 | 783 | 20.5 | 125 | 78.5 | 14.1 |
| Scottish Borders | 0.507 | 612 | 23.7 | 100 | 80.6 | 13.3 |
| Shetland Islands | 0.516 | 486 | 23.2 | 117 | 84.8 | 15.9 |
| South Ayrshire | 0.562 | 765 | 23.6 | 105 | 79.2 | 13.7 |
| South Lanarkshire | 0.676 | 793 | 21.7 | 125 | 78.4 | 14.5 |
| Stirling | 0.589 | 776 | 23.0 | 110 | 77.2 | 13.6 |
| West Dunbartonshire | 0.747 | 978 | 19.3 | 130 | 71.5 | 15.3 |
| West Lothian | 0.673 | 792 | 21.2 | 126 | 82.2 | 15.1 |
| | YES | COU | UNM | MOR | ACT | AGE |

Source: U.K. Office for National Statistics, the General Register Office for Scotland, the Scottish Office.

The systematic component here is **Xβ**, the stochastic component is **Y = YES**, and the link function is $\theta = -1/\mu$. One challenge with the analysis of these data is that there is relatively little variation through each of the variables in Table 4.3. In some senses, this is a good problem to have, but it makes it slightly more challenging to identify regional differentiation.

## 5. ESTIMATION PROCEDURES

### Estimation Techniques

This chapter develops the statistical computing technique used to produce maximum likelihood estimates for coefficients in generalized linear models: *iterative weighted least squares* (IWLS). All statistical software uses some iterative root-finding procedure to find maximum likelihood estimates; the advantage of iterative weighed least squares is that it finds these estimates for *any* generalized linear model specification based on an exponential family form (and a number of others as well, cf. Green, 1984). Nelder and Wedderburn (1972) proposed iteratively weighted least squares in their founding article as an integrating numerical technique for obtaining maximum likelihood coefficient estimates, and the GLIM package (Baker and Nelder, 1978) was the first to provide IWLS in a commercial form. All professional-level statistical computing implementations now employ IWLS to find maximum likelihood estimates for generalized linear models. To fully understand the numerical aspects of this technique, I first discuss finding coefficient estimates in nonlinear models (i.e., simple root finding), then I discuss weighted regression, and finally I discuss the iterating algorithm. This provides a background for understanding the special nature of reweighting estimation.

### Newton–Raphson and Root Finding

In most parametric data-analytic settings in the social sciences the problem of finding coefficient estimates given data and a model is equivalent to finding the most likely parameter value in the parameter space. For instance, in a simple binomial experiment where 10 flips of a coin produce five heads, the most likely value for the unknown but true probability of a heads is 0.5. In addition, 0.4 and 0.6 are slightly

less likely to be the underlying probability, 0.3 and 0.7 are even less likely, and so forth. So the problem of finding a maximally likely value of the unknown probability is equivalent to finding the mode of the function for the probability given the data over the parameter space, which happens to be [0, 1] in this case. This process as described is essentially maximum likelihood estimation.

In many settings, the problem of finding the best possible estimate for some coefficient value is simply finding a mode. In nonlinear models, we are often driven to use numerical techniques rather than well-developed theory. Numerical techniques in this context refer to the application of some algorithm that manipulates the data and the specified model to produce a mathematical solution for the modal point. Unlike well-proven *theoretical* approaches, such as that provided by least squares for linear models or the central limit theorem for simple sampling distributions, there is a certain amount of "messiness" inherent in numerical analysis due to machine-generated round-off and truncation in intermediate steps of the applied algorithm. Well-programmed numerical techniques recognize this state of affairs and are coded accordingly.

If we visualize the problem of numerical maximum likelihood estimation as that of finding the top of an "ant hill" in the parameter space, then it is easy to see that this is equivalent to finding the parameter value where the derivative of the likelihood function is equal to zero: where the tangent line is horizontal. Fortunately, many techniques have been developed by mathematicians to attack this problem. The most famous, and perhaps most widely used, is called Newton–Raphson and is based on (Sir Isaac) Newton's method for finding the roots of polynomial equations.

Newton's method is based on a Taylor series expansion around some given point. This is the principle that there exists a relationship between the value of a mathematical function (with continuous derivatives over the relevant support) at a given point, $x_0$, and the function value at another (perhaps close) point, $x_1$, given by

$$f(x_1) = f(x_0) + (x_1 - x_0)f'(x_0)$$
$$+ \frac{1}{2!}(x_1 - x_0)^2 f''(x_0) + \frac{1}{3!}(x_1 - x_0)^3 f'''(x_0) + \ldots,$$

where $f'$ is the first derivative with respect to $x$, $f''$ is the second derivative with respect to $x$, and so on. Infinite precision is achieved only with infinite application of the series (as opposed to just the four terms previously provided), and is therefore unobtainable. For the purposes of most statistical estimation, only the first two terms are required as a step in an iterative process. Note also that the rapidly growing factorial function in the denominator means that later terms will be unimportant.

Suppose we are interested in finding the point, $x_1$, such that $f(x_1) = 0$. This is a root of the function, $f(\ )$, in the sense that it provides a solution to the polynomial expressed by the function. It can also be thought of as the point where the function crosses the $x$-axis in a graph of $x$ versus $f(x)$. We could find this point using the Taylor series expansion in one step if we had an infinite precision calculator:

$$0 = f(x_0) + (x_1 - x_0)f'(x_0)$$
$$+ \frac{1}{2!}(x_1 - x_0)^2 f''(x_0) + \frac{1}{3!}(x_1 - x_0)^3 f''(x_0) + \dots .$$

Lacking that resource, it is clear from the additive nature of the Taylor series expansion that we could use some subset of the terms on the right-hand side to at least get *closer* to the desired point:

$$0 \cong f(x_0) + (x_1 - x_0)f'(x_0). \tag{5.1}$$

This shortcut is referred to as the Gauss-Newton method because it is based on Newton's algorithm, but leads to a least squares solution in multivariate problems. Newton's method rearranges (5.1) to produce at the $(j + 1)$th step,

$$x^{(j+1)} = x^{(j)} - \frac{f(x^{(j)})}{f'(x^{(j)})}, \tag{5.2}$$

so that progressively improved estimates are produced until $f(x^{(j+1)})$ is sufficiently close to zero. It is shown that this method converges rapidly (quadratically in fact) to a solution provided that the selected starting point is reasonably close to the solution. However, the results can be disastrous if this condition is not met.

The Newton–Raphson algorithm when applied to mode finding in a statistical setting adapts (5.1) to find the root of the *score function* (3.3): the first derivative of the log likelihood. First consider the single parameter estimation problem where we seek the mode of log likelihood function (3.2) from Chapter 3. If we treat the score function provided by (3.3) as the function of analysis from the Taylor expansion, then iterative estimates are produced by

$$\theta^{(j+1)} = \theta^{(j)} - \frac{\partial/\partial \theta l(\theta^{(j)}|\mathbf{y})}{\partial^2/\partial \theta \, \partial \theta' l(\theta^{(j)}|\mathbf{y})}. \tag{5.3}$$

Now generalize (5.3) by allowing multiple coefficients. The goal is to estimate a $k$-dimensional $\hat{\boldsymbol{\theta}}$ estimate given data and a model. The applicable multivariate likelihood updating equation is provided by

$$\boldsymbol{\theta}^{(j+1)} = \boldsymbol{\theta}^{(j)} - \frac{\partial}{\partial \boldsymbol{\theta}} l(\boldsymbol{\theta}^{(j)}|\mathbf{y}) \left( \frac{\partial^2}{\partial \boldsymbol{\theta} \, \partial \boldsymbol{\theta}'} l(\boldsymbol{\theta}^{(j)}|\mathbf{y}) \right)^{-1}. \tag{5.4}$$

Sometimes the Hessian matrix, $\mathbf{H} = \partial^2/\partial \boldsymbol{\theta} \, \partial \boldsymbol{\theta}' l(\boldsymbol{\theta}^{(j)}|\mathbf{y})$, is difficult to calculate and is replaced by its expectation with regard to $\boldsymbol{\theta}$, $\mathbf{A} = E_{\boldsymbol{\theta}}(\partial^2/\partial \boldsymbol{\theta} \, \partial \boldsymbol{\theta}' l(\boldsymbol{\theta}^{(j)}|\mathbf{y}))$. This modification is referred to as *Fisher scoring* (1925). For exponential family distributions and natural link functions (Table 4.1), the observed and expected Hessian matrix are identical (Fahrmeir & Tutz, 1994, p. 39; Lehmann & Casella, 1998, pp. 124–128).

At each step of the Newton–Raphson algorithm, a system of equations determined by the multivariate normal equations must be solved. This is of the form:

$$(\boldsymbol{\theta}^{(j+1)} - \boldsymbol{\theta}^{(j)})\mathbf{A} = -\frac{\partial}{\partial \boldsymbol{\theta}^{(j)}} l(\boldsymbol{\theta}^{(j)}|\mathbf{y}). \tag{5.5}$$

Given that there already exists a normal form, it is computationally convenient to solve on each iteration by least squares. Therefore the problem of mode finding reduces to a repeated weighted least squares application in which the inverse of the diagonal values of $\mathbf{A}$ are the appropriate weights. The next subsection describes weighted least squares in the general context.

*Weighted Least Squares*

The least squares estimate of linear model regression coefficients is produced by: $\hat{\boldsymbol{\beta}} = (\mathbf{X}'\mathbf{X})^{-1}\mathbf{X}'\mathbf{Y}$. This is not only a solution that minimizes the summed squared errors, $(\mathbf{Y} - \mathbf{X}\boldsymbol{\beta})'(\mathbf{Y} - \mathbf{X}\boldsymbol{\beta})$, but is also the maximum likelihood estimate. A standard technique for compensating for nonconstant error variance (heteroscedasticity) is to insert a diagonal matrix of weights, $\Omega$, into the calculation of $\hat{\beta}$ such that the heteroscedasticity is mitigated. The $\Omega$ matrix is created by taking the error variance of the $i$th case (estimated or known), $v_i$, and assigning the inverse to the $i$th diagonal: $\Omega_{ii} = 1/v_i$. The idea is that large error variances are reduced by multiplication of the reciprocal.

To further explain this idea of weighted regression, begin with the standard linear model from (1.2):

$$Y_i = X_i\beta + \epsilon_i. \tag{5.6}$$

Now observe that there is heteroscedasticity in the error term so: $\epsilon_i = \epsilon v_i$, where the shared (minimum) variance is $\epsilon$ (i.e., nonindexed), and differences are reflected in the $v_i$ term. To give a trivial, but instructive, example, visualize a heteroscedastic error vector: $E = [1, 2, 3, 4]$. Then $\epsilon = 1$, and the $v$-vector is $v = [1, 2, 3, 4]$. So by the earlier logic, the $\Omega$ matrix for this example is:

$$\Omega = \begin{bmatrix} \frac{1}{v_1} & 0 & 0 & 0 \\ 0 & \frac{1}{v_2} & 0 & 0 \\ 0 & 0 & \frac{1}{v_3} & 0 \\ 0 & 0 & 0 & \frac{1}{v_4} \end{bmatrix} = \begin{bmatrix} 1 & 0 & 0 & 0 \\ 0 & \frac{1}{2} & 0 & 0 \\ 0 & 0 & \frac{1}{3} & 0 \\ 0 & 0 & 0 & \frac{1}{4} \end{bmatrix}.$$

We can premultiply each term in (5.6), by the square root of the $\Omega$ matrix (that is by the standard deviation). This "square root" is actually produced from a Cholesky factorization: if $A$ is a positive definite,[10] symmetric ($A' = A$) matrix, then there must exist a matrix $G$ such that: $A = GG'$. In our case, this decomposition is greatly simplified because the $\Omega$ matrix has only diagonal values (all off-diagonal values equal to zero). Therefore the Cholesky factorization is produced simply from the square root of these diagonal values. Premultiplying (5.6) as such, gives:

$$\Omega^{1/2}Y_i = \Omega^{1/2}X_i\beta + \Omega^{1/2}\epsilon_i. \tag{5.7}$$

So if the heteroscedasticity in the error term is expressed as the diagonals of a matrix: $\epsilon \sim (0, \sigma^2 V)$, then (5.7) gives: $\epsilon \sim (0, \Omega\sigma^2 V) = (0, \sigma^2)$, and the heteroscedasticity is removed. Now instead of minimizing $(Y - X\beta)'(Y - X\beta)$, we minimize

$(\mathbf{Y} - \mathbf{X\beta})'\mathbf{\Omega}^{-1}(\mathbf{Y} - \mathbf{X\beta})$, and the weighted least squares estimator is found by $\hat{\boldsymbol{\beta}} = (\mathbf{X'\Omega X})^{-1}\mathbf{X'\Omega Y}$. The latter result is found by rearranging (5.7). The weighted least squares estimator gives the best linear unbiased estimate (BLUE) of the coefficient estimator in the presence of heteroscedasticity. Note also that if the residuals are homoscedastic, then the weights are simply 1 and (5.7) reduces to (5.6).

*Iterative Weighted Least Squares*

Suppose that the individual variances used to make the reciprocal diagonal values for $\mathbf{\Omega}$ are unknown and cannot be easily estimated, but it is known that they are a function of the mean of the outcome variable: $v_i = f(E[Y_i])$. So if the expected value of the outcome variable, $E[Y_i] = \mu$, and the form of the relation function, $f(\ )$, are known then this is a very straightforward estimation procedure. Unfortunately, even though it is very common for the variance structure to be dependent on the mean function, it is relatively rare to know the exact form of the dependence.

A solution to this problem is to iteratively estimate the weights, improving the estimate on each cycle using the mean function. Since $\mu = g^{-1}(\mathbf{X\beta})$, then the coefficient estimate, $\hat{\boldsymbol{\beta}}$, provides a mean estimate and vice versa. So the algorithm iteratively estimates these quantities using progressively improving weights. This proceeds as follows:

1. Assign starting values to the weights, generally equal to one (i.e., unweighted regression): $1/v_i^{(1)} = 1$, and construct the diagonal matrix $\mathbf{\Omega}$, guarding against division by zero.

2. Estimate $\boldsymbol{\beta}$ using weighted least squares with the current weights. The $j$th estimate is: $\hat{\boldsymbol{\beta}}^{(j)} = (\mathbf{X'\Omega}^{(j)}\mathbf{X})^{-1}\mathbf{X'\Omega}^{(j)}\mathbf{Y}$.

3. Update the weights using the new estimated mean vector: $1/v_i^{(j+1)} = \text{VAR}(\mu_i)$.

4. Repeat steps 2 and 3 until convergence (i.e., $\mathbf{X}\hat{\boldsymbol{\beta}}^{(j)} - \mathbf{X}\hat{\boldsymbol{\beta}}^{(j+1)}$ is sufficiently close to zero).

Under very general conditions, satisfied by the exponential family of distributions, the iterative weighted least squares procedure finds the mode of the likelihood function, thus producing the maximum likelihood estimate of the unknown coefficient vector, $\hat{\boldsymbol{\beta}}$. Furthermore, the matrix produced by: $\hat{\sigma}^2(\mathbf{X'\Omega X})^{-1}$ converges in probability to the variance matrix of $\hat{\boldsymbol{\beta}}$ as desired.

Because we have an explicit link function identified in a generalized linear model, the form of the multivariate normal equation (5.8) is modified to include this embedded transformation:

$$(\theta^{(j+1)} - \theta^{(j)})\mathbf{A} = -\frac{\partial l(\theta^{(j)}|\mathbf{y})}{\partial g^{-1}(\theta)} \frac{\partial g^{-1}(\theta)}{\partial(\theta)}. \tag{5.8}$$

Its easy to see that in the case of the linear model, when the link is just the identity function, that (5.8) simplifies to (5.5). The overall strategy of the IWLS procedure for generalized linear models is fairly simple: Newton–Raphson with Fisher scoring applied iteratively to the modified normal equation (5.8). For excellent detailed analyses and extensions of this procedure, the reader is directed to Green (1984) and del Pino (1989).

*Example 5.1: Poisson Generalized Linear Model of Capital Punishment, Continued.* Returning to the problem of modeling the application of capital punishment at the state-wide level in the United States, we now implement the iterative weighted least squares algorithm to produce the desired $\hat{\boldsymbol{\beta}}$ coefficients in $E[\mathbf{Y}] = g^{-1}(\mathbf{X}\hat{\boldsymbol{\beta}})$. This produces the output in Table 5.1.

The iterative weighted least squares algorithm converged in three iterations in this example partly due to the simplicity of the example

TABLE 5.1
Modeling Capital Punishment in the United States: 1997

|  | Coefficient | Standard Error | 95% Confidence Interval |
|---|---|---|---|
| (Intercept) | −6.30665 | 4.17678 | [−14.49299: 1.87969] |
| Median income | 0.00027 | 0.00005 | [ 0.00017: 0.00037] |
| Percent poverty | 0.06897 | 0.07979 | [ −0.08741: 0.22534] |
| Percent Black | −0.09500 | 0.02284 | [ −0.13978: −0.05023] |
| log(Violent crime) | 0.22124 | 0.44243 | [ −0.64591: 1.08838] |
| South | 2.30988 | 0.42875 | [ 1.46955: 3.15022] |
| Degree proportion | −19.70241 | 4.46366 | [−28.45102:−10.95380] |

Null deviance: 136.573, $df = 16$     Maximized $l(\ )$: −31.7375
Summed deviance: 18.212, $df = 11$     AIC: 77.475

and partly due to the well-behaved structure of the likelihood surface. The standard errors are calculated from the square root of the diagonal of the variance–covariance matrix which is the negative inverse of the expected Hessian matrix discussed previously: $\mathbf{A} = E(\partial^2/\partial\boldsymbol{\theta}\,\partial\boldsymbol{\theta}'l(\boldsymbol{\theta}^{(j)}|\mathbf{y}))$. Since the expected Hessian calculation is used in this example, the estimation algorithm is Fisher scoring. The variance–covariance matrix is often useful in these settings for determining the existence of problems such as multicollinearity (large off-diagonal values) and near-nonidentifiability (rows or columns with all values equal to or near zero). The variance covariance matrix in this problem shows no signs of such pathologies:

$$\mathbf{VC} = (-\mathbf{A})^{-1} =$$

| Int | INC | POV |
|---|---|---|
| 17.445501654 | −0.000131052 | −0.198325558 |
| −0.000131052 | 0.000000003 | 0.000001862 |
| −0.198325558 | 0.000001862 | 0.006365688 |
| 0.017689695 | 0.000000113 | 0.000158039 |
| −1.484011921 | 0.000004171 | 0.003911954 |
| 0.368916884 | −0.000006245 | −0.017825119 |
| −4.651658695 | −0.000094858 | 0.121451892 |

| BLK | log(CRI) | SOU | DEG |
|---|---|---|---|
| 0.017689695 | −1.484011921 | 0.368916884 | −4.651658695 |
| 0.000000113 | 0.000004171 | −0.000006245 | −0.000094858 |
| 0.000158039 | 0.003911954 | −0.017825119 | 0.121451892 |
| 0.000521871 | −0.003283494 | −0.005090192 | −0.033679253 |
| −0.003283494 | 0.195742167 | −0.001384018 | 0.397439934 |
| −0.005090192 | −0.001384018 | 0.183825030 | 0.298730196 |
| −0.033679253 | 0.397439934 | 0.298730196 | 19.924250374 |

Several interesting substantive conclusions are provided by this model. The coefficient for percent of poverty in the state, and the previous year's log-crime rate have 95% confidence intervals that bound zero. So there is no evidence provided by this model and these data that the rate of executions is tied to poverty levels or the preceding year's crime rate. These are often used as explanations for higher murder rates and therefore presumably higher execution rates. However, higher income and education levels both have 95% confidence intervals bounded away from zero (far away in fact). The coefficient for income is positively signed inferring that higher levels of income are associated with more executions. Interestingly, states with higher education levels tend to have fewer executions. It has been suggested that increased education (generally at the university level) can provide a distaste for capital punishment.

The negative sign on the coefficient for percent Black population is also interesting as it has a 95% confidence interval bounded away from zero. One possible explanation is linked to the preponderance of evidence that the death penalty is applied disproportionately to Black prisoners (Baldus & Cole, 1980). The large and positive coefficient indicating that a state is in the South is not surprising given the history of capital punishment in that region of the country.

Two admonitions are warranted at this point. First, note that 95% confidence intervals are provided in Table 5.1 rather than $t$-statistics and $p$-values. Actually, the four coefficients with 95% confidence intervals bounded away from zero in this model could have reported 99.9% confidence intervals bounded away from zero if it were important to provide such a finding. The use of confidence intervals rather than $p$-values or "stars" throughout the text is done to avoid the common misinterpretations of these devices that are prevalent in the social sciences (Gill, 1999). Confidence intervals provide *all* of the information that $p$ values would supply: a 95% confidence interval bounded away from zero is functionally equivalent to a $p$-value lower than 0.05.

Second, the coefficients in Table 5.1 should not be interpreted like linear model coefficients: a one unit change in the $k$th explanatory variable value *does not* provide a $\beta_k$ change in the outcome variable because the relationship is expressed through the nonlinear link function. A more appropriate interpretation is to look at *first differences*: analyzing outcome variable differences at two researcher determined levels of some explanatory variable value. In the capital punishment example, if we hold all the explanatory variables constant at their mean except for the dummy variable indicating whether or not the state is in the South, then the first difference for this dummy variable is: 8.156401. This means that there is an expected increase of about eight executions per year just because a state is in the South. It should be noted, as we see later when discussing residuals, that the Texas case is driving this finding to a great degree.

Figure 5.1 provides another way of looking at the output from the Poisson generalized linear model (GLM) model of capital punishment. In this graphical display the expected count of executions is

48

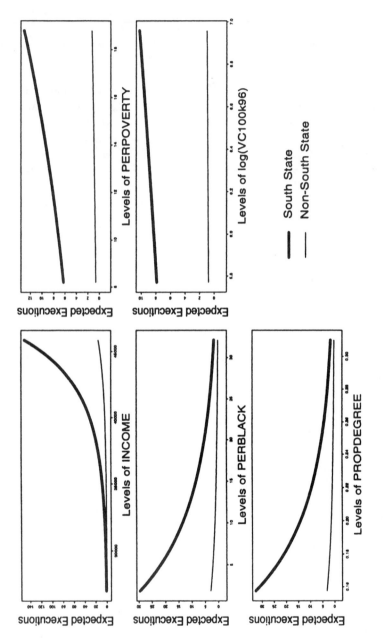

Figure 5.1. Controlling for the South: Capital punishment model.

plotted along the $Y$-axis and each of the explanatory variables is plotted over its observed range along the $X$-axis with the dummy variable either off (thin line) or on (thick line). The variables not displayed in a particular graph are held constant at their mean. In this way, we can see how changes in a specified explanatory factor differ in affecting the outcome variable depending on the status of the dichotomous variable, controlling for the others. For example, in Panel 1, we see that as income increases, the expected number of executions increases only slightly for non-South states but increases dramatically and seemingly exponentially for states in the South.

There is a similar effect apparent between panels 3 and 5. As both the percentage of blacks and the education level increases, the expected number of executions for states in the South dramatically decreases until it nearly converges with non-South states at the upper limit. Note that this approach provides far more information than simply observing that the sign on the coefficient estimate is negative.

*Example 5.2: Gamma Generalized Linear Model of Electoral Politics in Scotland, Continued.* Returning to the Scottish voting example discussed in Chapter 4, we now run the generalized linear model with the gamma link function, $\theta = -1/\mu$. This produces the output in Table 5.2.

TABLE 5.2
Modeling the Vote for Parliamentary Taxation: 1997

|  | Coefficient | Standard Error | 95% Confidence Interval |
|---|---|---|---|
| (Intercept) | −1.77653 | 1.14789 | [−4.14566: 0.59261] |
| Council tax | 0.00496 | 0.00162 | [ 0.00162: 0.00831] |
| Female unemployment | 0.20344 | 0.05321 | [ 0.09363: 0.31326] |
| Standardized mortality | −0.00718 | 0.00271 | [−0.01278:−0.00159] |
| Economically active | 0.01119 | 0.00406 | [ 0.00281: 0.01956] |
| GDP | −0.00001 | 0.00001 | [−0.00004: 0.00001] |
| Percent aged 5–15 | −0.05187 | 0.02403 | [−0.10145:−0.00228] |
| Council tax: Female un. | −0.00024 | 0.00007 | [−0.00040:−0.00009] |

Null deviance: 0.536072, $df = 31$      Maximized $l(\ ): 63.89$
Summed deviance: 0.087389, $df = 24$      AIC: −111.78

The iterative weighted least squares algorithm converged in two iterations in this example. The dispersion parameter, $a(\phi) = 1/\delta$, is estimated to be 0.003584. We use this information when we return to this example in the following text during the discussion of residuals and model fit. In addition, an interaction term between the council tax variable and the female unemployment variables is added to the model. This is done in exactly the same way as in standard linear models. Here it shows some evidence that increasing amounts of council taxes are associated with a decrease in the slope of female unemployment change. It should be noted that no causality is thus asserted.

The resulting model has a number of interesting findings. First, it is surprising that the gross domestic product (GDP) is not 95% confidence interval (CI) bounded away from zero (i.e., not statistically significant at the $p < 0.05$ level). One would think that the level of economic production in a given region would shape attitudes about taxation policy and taxation authority, but there is no evidence of that effect from these data and this model. The other economic variable, the current level of the council tax, does have a coefficient that is 95% CI bounded away from zero. The sign is positive suggesting that council districts with higher taxes (such as Glasgow) see parliamentary taxation as a potential substitute for an uneven levy that currently disadvantages them. Also, the higher taxed districts are generally more urban, and it could be that urban voters rather than higher taxed voters have a greater preference for parliamentary taxation authority (although this claim is not specifically tested here).

Each of the social variables has a 95% CI bounded away from zero, and the model clearly favors these social effects over economic effects as explanations of the vote. Both employment related variables are signed positively, which is a little befuddling. Higher levels of unemployment, as measured through female applications for benefits, are associated with greater support for the new taxation authority. Yet higher levels of working age individuals participating in the economy are also associated with greater support. The mortality index is negatively signed, which seems to imply that older constituencies are less enthusiastic about parliamentary taxation or perhaps more inclined toward tradition. Finally, those districts with higher numbers of children in the 5–15 range are less likely to support the proposition. Since the current council tax provides breaks for families with children, this could be a concern that some new tax scheme in the future might have different priorities.

The quality of the fit of the model developed in this example will be analyzed in the following text. In the interim, one quick indication is that all but one of the explanatory variables has a 95% confidence interval bounded away from zero.

## 6. RESIDUALS AND MODEL FIT

### Defining Residuals

Residuals (errors, disturbances) are typically analyzed in linear modeling with the goal of identifying poorly fitting values. If it is observed that there exist a sufficiently large number of these poorly fitting values, then often the linear fit is determined to be inappropriate for the data. Other common uses of residuals include: looking for signs of nonlinearity, evaluating the effect of new explanatory variables, creating goodness of fit statistics, and evaluating leverage (distance from the mean) and influence (change exerted on the coefficient) for individual data points.

Because of the generalization to a wider class of outcome variable forms, residuals in generalized linear models are often not normally distributed and therefore require a more careful analysis. Despite this challenge, we would very much like to have a form of the residuals from a generalized linear model that is as close as possible to normally distributed around zero, or at least "nearly identically distributed" in Cox and Snell's language (1968). The motivation is that we can then apply a wide range of graphical and inferential tools developed for the linear model to investigate potential outliers and other interesting behavior. The core emphasis in this chapter is the discussion of *Anscombe* and *deviance* residuals which are attempts to describe the stochastic behavior of the data relative to a constructed generalized linear model in a format that closely resembles the normal theory analysis of standard linear model residuals.

Actually, five different types of residuals are used with generalized linear models and are discussed in this chapter: response, Pearson, working, Anscombe, and deviance. For the standard linear model these forms are equivalent. However, for other exponential family forms, they can differ substantially and confusingly.

A substantial advantage of the generalized linear model is its freedom from the standard Gauss–Markov assumption that the residuals have mean zero and constant variance. Yet this freedom comes with the price of interpreting more complex stochastic structures. Currently, the dominant philosophy is to assess this stochastic element by looking at (summed) discrepancies: a function that describes the difference between observed and expected outcome data for some specified model: $D = \sum_{i=1}^{n} d(\theta, y_i)$. This definition is left intentionally vague for the moment to stress that the format of $D$ is widely applicable. For instance, if the discrepancy in $D$ is measured as the squared arithmetic difference from a single mean, then this becomes the standard form for the variance. In terms of generalized linear models, the squared difference from the mean will prove to be an overly restrictive definition of discrepancy, and a likelihood-based measure will show to be far more useful.

For the standard linear model, the residual vector is not only quite easy to calculate, it also plays a central role in determining the quality of fit of the model. The *response* residual vector, is calculated simply as $\mathbf{R}_{\text{Response}} = \mathbf{Y} - \mathbf{X}\boldsymbol{\beta}$ and is used to measure both the dispersion around the fitted line, and the level of compliance with the Gauss–Markov assumptions. As applied to generalized linear models, the linear predictor needs to be transformed by the link function to be comparable with the response vector. Therefore, the response residual vector for generalized linear models is: $\mathbf{R}_{\text{Response}} = \mathbf{Y} - g^{-1}(\mathbf{X}\boldsymbol{\beta})$.

It is seldom mentioned in introductory texts, but the linear model is moderately robust to minor deviations from the standard assumptions. Individual cases in social science data sets are not uncommonly correlated in some relatively mild or benign fashion. Sometimes there will be large outliers with or without influence (individually causing nontrivial change in the estimated slopes). In many of these situations the substantive conclusions are barely affected or at least minimally affected in comparison to the assumed effects of measurement error. Furthermore, asymptotic normality of the residuals is still achievable in a more general setting by appealing to the Lindeburg–Feller variant of the central limit theorem. This theorem relaxes casewise independence in favor of the condition that no single term dominates in the sum. However, it is far more typical with generalized linear models to produce residuals which deviate substantially rather than mildly from the basic conditions. In these cases, response residuals tell us very little.

A basic alternative to the standard response residual is the *Pearson residual*. This is the response residual scaled by the standard deviation of the prediction:

$$R_{\text{Pearson}} = \frac{Y - \mu}{\sqrt{\text{VAR}[\mu]}}.$$

Pearson residuals are an attempt to provide some sense of scale to the response residual by dividing by the standard error of the prediction. The name comes from the fact that the sum of the Pearson residuals for a Poisson generalized linear model is the Pearson $\chi^2$ goodness of fit measure reported by all statistical packages. In ideal and asymptotic situations, the Pearson residuals are normally distributed. Unfortunately, like response residuals, Pearson residuals can be very skewed, and can therefore provide a misleading measure of typical dispersion.

In the process of fitting generalized linear models, software programs use the iterative weighted least squares algorithm. As described in Chapter 5, a set of working weights is calculated at each step of a linear estimation until the appropriate derivative is sufficiently close to zero. An occasionally useful quantity is the residual produced from the last (i.e., determining) step of the iterative weighting process: the difference between the current working response and the linear predictor. This is defined as

$$R_{\text{Working}} = (y - \mu)\frac{\partial}{\partial \theta}\mu.$$

This residual is sometimes used as a diagnostic for evaluating convergence as well as an indication of model fit at this point. A lack of general theory for working residuals hampers their use in a more broad context.

*Anscombe Residuals*

One imaginative strategy to compensate for the nonnormality problems with Pearson residuals is to alter both terms in the numerator of the Pearson residual such that the residuals are distributed as close to normally as possible (Anscombe, 1960, 1961). The idea is to transform the residuals in such a way that first-order asymptotic skewness is mitigated and the form is approximately unimodal and symmetric.

This new function, $A(y)$, is given by

$$A(y) = \int \text{VAR}[\mu]^{-1/3} \, d\mu, \qquad (6.1)$$

where $\text{VAR}[\mu]$ is the variance function from Chapter 3 expressed in terms of $\mu$. The Anscombe residual applies this function to both $Y$ and $\mu$, adjusting for the scale of the variance to normalize by dividing with

$$\frac{\partial}{\partial \mu} A(y) \sqrt{\tau^2}, \qquad (6.2)$$

using the definition of $\tau^2$ from Table 3.1 in Chapter 3. This solution therefore uses differential equations to mimic normality to the greatest extent possible. There is a maddeningly great diversity of the forms that the Anscombe residuals take in the literature (McCullagh & Nelder, 1989, p. 38; Fahrmeir & Tutz, 1994, p. 132; Pierce & Schafer, 1986, p. 978; and Cox & Snell, 1968, pp. 258–261). A partial explanation for this diversity of forms is the desire of a number of authors to "smooth" the estimates toward the mean by adding or subtracting a constant to integer values in a manner similar to Yates' correction factor in chi-square tests of independence. This will not produce a noticeable difference, however, with large sample sizes. There are also a number of bias-correcting strategies of varying complexity and usefulness. This monograph takes the position of McCullagh and Nelder (1989), that the simplest form is the best at this level, and drops these enhancements for the sake of parsimony rather than as a criticism of such approaches.

Table 6.1 shows the production of Anscombe residuals for the running example exponential family forms. Following McCullagh and Nelder (1989), constants are dropped out before the differential equation calculations since they cancel in the final step anyway. The Anscombe residual form for the standard linear model is not included in Table 6.1 since these residuals are already normal by construct.

The development of the binomial transformation in Table 6.1 differs from the described procedure. Directly applying the $A(y) = \int (\text{VAR}[\mu])^{-1/3} \, d\mu$ integral leads to the incomplete beta function: $B_x(a, b) = \int_0^x t^{a-1}(1 - t)^{b-1} \, dt$, which is analytically intractable and difficult to numerically tabulate. Cox and Snell (1968) use the trick

TABLE 6.1
Anscombe Residuals

| | | |
|---|---|---|
| Poisson | $A(y)$ | $\int (\text{VAR}[\mu])^{-1/3} \, d\mu = \int (\mu)^{-1/3} \, d\mu = \frac{3}{2}\mu^{2/3}$ |
| | $\frac{\partial}{\partial\mu} A(y)\sqrt{\tau^2}$ | $\frac{\partial}{\partial\mu} A(y)\sqrt{\tau^2} = \left[\frac{\partial}{\partial\mu} \frac{3}{2}\mu^{2/3}\right]\sqrt{\mu} = \mu^{1/6}$ |
| | $R_A$ | $\frac{3}{2}\left(y^{2/3} - \mu^{2/3}\right)/\mu^{1/6}$ |
| Binomial | $A(y)$ | $\phi(\mu) = \int_0^\mu t^{-1/3}(1 - t)^{-1/3} = I_\mu\left(\frac{2}{3}, \frac{2}{3}\right) B\left(\frac{2}{3}, \frac{2}{3}\right)$ |
| | | $\mu_i^{1/6}(1 - \mu_i)^{1/6}$ |
| | $R_A$ | $\left(\phi\left(\frac{Y_i}{m_i}\right) - \phi(\mu_i)\right)\mu_i^{1/6}(1 - \mu_i)^{1/6}$ |
| Gamma | $A(y)$ | $\int (\text{VAR}[\mu])^{-1/3} \, d\mu = \int (\mu^2)^{-1/3} \, d\mu = 3\mu^{1/3}$ |
| | $\frac{\partial}{\partial\mu} A(y)\sqrt{\tau^2}$ | $\left[\frac{\partial}{\partial\mu} 3\mu^{1/6}\right]\mu = \mu^{1/3}$ |
| | $R_A$ | $3(y^{1/3} - \mu^{1/3})/\mu^{1/3}$ |
| Negative binomial | $A(y)$ | $\phi(\mu) = \int_0^\mu t^{-1/3}(1 - t)^{-1/3} \, d\mu = I_\mu\left(\frac{2}{3}, \frac{2}{3}\right) B\left(\frac{2}{3}, \frac{2}{3}\right)$ |
| | | $\mu_i^{1/6}(1 - \mu_i)^{1/6}$ |
| | $R_A$ | $\left(\phi\left(\frac{r_i}{Y_i}\right) - \phi(\mu_i)\right)\mu_i^{1/6}(1 - \mu_i)^{1/6}$ |

that by dividing the incomplete beta function, $\phi(\mu)$, by the complete beta function, $B(a, b) = \Gamma(a)\Gamma(b)/\Gamma(a + b)$ (where the gamma function is the continuous analog of the discrete factorial notation: "!"), one gets a symmetric form which is easier to tabulate[11] (Cox & Snell, p. 260). Furthermore, they find that the normalizing factor in the denominator has excellent empirical properties, although no specific theoretical justification is given.

The binomial form in Table 6.1 contrasts the empirical outcomes: $Y_i/m_i$, the number of successes in $m$ trials per case, and the contribution from the systematic component through the link function: $\mu_i$. For clarification of the process for obtaining binomial Anscombe residuals, consider the hypothetical example in which $y_i/m_i = 0.12$, and $\mu_i = 0.24$. Using the Cox and Snell table, we can look up the values: $I_{0.12} = 0.181$, $I_{0.24} = 0.292$. The Anscombe residual then is produced by:

$$\phi\left(\frac{y_i}{m_i}\right) = I_{0.12}\left(\frac{2}{3}, \frac{2}{3}\right) B\left(\frac{2}{3}, \frac{2}{3}\right)$$

$$= (0.181)(2.05339) = 0.3716636,$$

$$\phi(\mu_i) = I_{0.24}\left(\frac{2}{3}, \frac{2}{3}\right) B\left(\frac{2}{3}, \frac{2}{3}\right)$$

$$= (0.292)(2.05339) = 0.5995899,$$

$$\mu_i^{1/6}(1 - \mu_i)^{1/6} = (0.24)^{1/6}(1 - 0.24)^{1/6} = 0.7530737,$$

$$R_A = \frac{0.3716636 - 0.5995899}{0.7530737} = -0.3026613.$$

The literature on Anscombe residuals contains no direct discussion of the negative binomial PMF. The prescribed negative binomial $A(y)$ integral produces an even more unpleasant form than the binomial: $\int(\mu^{-2} - \mu^{-1})^{1/3} d\mu$. The recommendation is to appeal to similarity with the binomial distribution and adapt the Cox and Snell approach. Suppose that $X_1$ is a distributed binomial with $n$ trials and probability $p$, and $X_2$ is a distributed negative binomial with $r$ successes desired and probability $p$. Then the cumulative distribution functions are equivalent at the points $r - 1$ and $n - r$ at these points: $F_{X_1}(r - 1) = F_{X_2}(n - r)$ (Casella & Berger, 1990, p. 123), and this can be thought of as the point where a series of hypothetically consecutive failures end. Based on this equivalence, an argument can be made to treat these Anscombe residuals equivalently. This approach is taken in Table 6.1, where the only difference is the probability determination in the numerator.

### The Deviance Function and Deviance Residuals

By far the most useful category of residuals for the generalized linear model is the deviance residual. This is also the most general form. A common way to look at model specification is the analysis of the likelihood ratio statistic comparing a proposed model specification relative to the saturated model ($n$ data points, $n$ specified parameters, using the exact same data and link function). The difference in fit is generally called the summed deviance. Since this deviance is composed of the contributions from each data point and the difference between summarizing with a relatively small subset of parameters and one parameter for every data point, then these individual deviances are directly analogous to residuals.

Starting with the log likelihood for a proposed model from the (3.2) notation, add the " ˆ " notation as a reminder that it is evaluated at the maximum likelihood values:

$$l(\hat{\boldsymbol{\theta}}, \psi | \mathbf{y}) = \sum_{i=1}^{n} \frac{y_i \hat{\boldsymbol{\theta}} - b(\hat{\boldsymbol{\theta}})}{a(\psi)} + c(\mathbf{y}, \psi).$$

Also, consider the same log likelihood function with the same data and the same link function, except that it now has $n$ coefficients for the $n$ data points, i.e., the saturated model log likelihood function with the " ˜ " function to denote the $n$-length $\boldsymbol{\theta}$ vector:

$$l(\tilde{\boldsymbol{\theta}}, \psi | \mathbf{y}) = \sum_{i=1}^{n} \frac{y_i \tilde{\boldsymbol{\theta}} - b(\tilde{\boldsymbol{\theta}})}{a(\psi)} + c(\mathbf{y}, \psi).$$

This is the highest possible value for the log likelihood function achievable with the given data, $\mathbf{y}$. Yet it is also often unhelpful analytically except as a benchmark. The deviance function is defined as minus twice the log likelihood ratio (that is the arithmetic difference since both terms are already written on the log metric):

$$
\begin{aligned}
D(\boldsymbol{\theta}, \mathbf{y}) &= -2 \sum_{i=1}^{n} \left[ l(\tilde{\boldsymbol{\theta}}, \psi | \mathbf{y}) - l(\hat{\boldsymbol{\theta}}, \psi | \mathbf{y}) \right] \\
&= -2 \sum_{i=1}^{n} \left[ \left( \frac{y_i \tilde{\boldsymbol{\theta}} - b(\tilde{\boldsymbol{\theta}})}{a(\psi)} + c(\mathbf{y}, \psi) \right) \right. \\
&\qquad \left. - \left( \frac{y_i \hat{\boldsymbol{\theta}} - b(\hat{\boldsymbol{\theta}})}{a(\psi)} + c(\mathbf{y}, \psi) \right) \right] \\
&= -2 \sum_{i=1}^{n} \left[ y_i (\tilde{\boldsymbol{\theta}} - \hat{\boldsymbol{\theta}}) - (b(\tilde{\boldsymbol{\theta}}) - b(\hat{\boldsymbol{\theta}})) \right] a(\psi)^{-1}. \quad (6.3)
\end{aligned}
$$

Sometimes this deviance function (or summed deviance) is indexed by a weighting factor, $w_i$, to accommodate grouped data. Also, when

$a(\psi)$ is included (6.3) is called the *scaled* deviance function; otherwise it is predictably called *unscaled*.

This is a measure of the summed difference of the data-weighted maximum likelihood estimates and the $b(\theta)$ parameters. Thus the deviation function gives a measure of the trade-off between a saturated model which fits every single data point, assigning all variation to the systematic component, and a proposed model which reflects the researcher's belief about the identification of the systematic and random components. Hypothesis tests of fit are performed using the asymptotic property that $D(\theta, y) \sim \chi^2_{n-k}$ (although the asymptotic rate of convergence varies dramatically depending on the exponential family form). Observe also that the $b(\theta)$ function developed in Chapter 2 plays a critical role once again.

Although calculating $D(\theta, y)$ is relatively straightforward, we usually do not need to develop this calculation as many texts provide the result for frequently used PDFs and PMFs. For the running examples, the deviance functions are given in Table 6.2.

A utility of the deviance function is that it also allows a look at the individual deviance contributions in an analogous way to linear model residuals. The single point deviance function is just the deviance function for the $y_i$th point (i.e., without the summation):

$$d(\theta, y_i) = -2\Big[y_i(\tilde{\theta} - \hat{\theta}) - \big(b(\tilde{\theta}) - b(\hat{\theta})\big)\Big]a(\psi)^{-1}.$$

TABLE 6.2
Deviance Functions

| Distribution | Canonical Parameter | Deviance Function |
|---|---|---|
| Poisson $(\mu)$ | $\theta = \log(\mu)$ | $2\sum\Big[y_i \log\big(\frac{y_i}{\mu_i}\big) - y_i + \mu_i\Big]$ |
| Binomial $(m, p)$ | $\theta = \log\big(\frac{\mu}{1-\mu}\big)$ | $2\sum\Big[y_i \log\big(\frac{y_i}{\mu_i}\big) + (m_i - y_i)\log\big(\frac{m_i - y_i}{m_i - \mu_i}\big)\Big]$ |
| Normal $(\mu, \sigma)$ | $\theta = \mu$ | $\sum[y_i - \mu_i]^2$ |
| Gamma $(\mu, \delta)$ | $\theta = -\frac{1}{\mu}$ | $2\sum\Big[-\log\big(\frac{y_i}{\mu_i}\big) + \frac{y_i - \mu_i}{\mu_i}\Big]$ |
| Negative binomial $(\mu, p)$ | $\theta = \log(1 - \mu)$ | $2\sum\Big[y_i \log\big(\frac{y_i}{\mu_i}\big) + (1 + y_i)\log\big(\frac{1 + \mu_i}{1 + y_i}\big)\Big]$ |

To define the deviance residual at the $y_i$ point, we take the square root,

$$\mathbf{R}_{\text{Deviance}} = \frac{(y_i - \mu_i)}{|y_i - \mu_i|} \sqrt{|d(\theta, y_i)|},$$

where $(y_i - \mu_i)/|y_i - \mu_i|$ is just a sign-preserving function.

Pierce and Schafer (1986) study the deviance residual in detail and recommend that a continuity correction of $E_\theta[(y_i - \mu_i)/\text{VAR}[y_i]]^3$ be added to each term in the right-hand column of Table 6.2 to improve the normal approximation. Furthermore, in the case of binomial, negative binomial, and Poisson exponential family forms, they prescribe adding or subtracting $\frac{1}{2}$ to integer valued $y_i$ outcomes to move these values toward the mean. These are then called *adjusted deviances*.

Despite completely different derivations, Anscombe and deviance residuals behave in a surprisingly similar fashion. This is because in both cases the goal was normality. In general, these two approaches are quite successful in producing residual structures that are: centered at zero, have standard error of one, and are approximately normal.

*Example 6.1: Poisson Generalized Linear Model of Capital Punishment, Continued.* Returning once again to the Poisson-based example using 1997 capital punishment data in the United States, we now look at various residuals from the model. These data were chosen specifically because there is one case with a noticeably large outcome variable value: Texas. This makes the residuals analysis particularly interesting given the perceived dominance by this one case. Table 6.3 provides the residual vectors for each type studied.

Note from Table 6.3 that in no single case does the sign of the residual change across residual types. If a change of sign were observed, a coding error should be suspected. The table also reinforces the point that deviance and Anscombe residuals are not very different in practice although they look very different in theory. In addition, the Pearson residuals are not very different from the deviance or Anscombe residuals in this example except for one point (Missouri) producing a notable skewness, exactly as the theoretical discussion predicted for Pearson residuals. The large, positive residuals for Missouri indicate that it has more executions than expected given the observed levels of the explanatory variables.

TABLE 6.3
Residuals From the Poisson Model of Capital Punishment

|  | Response | Pearson | Working | Deviance | Anscombe |
|---|---|---|---|---|---|
| Texas | 1.70755431 | 0.28741478 | 0.04837752 | 0.28515874 | .28292493 |
| Virginia | 0.87407687 | 0.30671010 | 0.10762321 | 0.30136452 | 0.29629097 |
| Missouri | 4.59530299 | 3.86395636 | 3.24898061 | 2.86925916 | 2.27854829 |
| Arkansas | 0.26481208 | 0.13694108 | 0.07081505 | 0.13544624 | 0.13391171 |
| Alabama | 0.95958171 | 0.67097152 | 0.46916278 | 0.62736060 | 0.58874967 |
| Arizona | 0.95395198 | 0.93375106 | 0.91397549 | 0.82741022 | 0.74425671 |
| Illinois | 0.13924315 | 0.10197129 | 0.07467388 | 0.10084230 | 0.09963912 |
| South Carolina | -0.38227185 | -0.24752186 | -0.16027167 | -0.25478237 | -0.26235519 |
| Colorado | -0.95901329 | -0.68428704 | -0.48826435 | -0.75706323 | -0.84845827 |
| Florida | -1.82216650 | -1.08543456 | -0.64657649 | -1.25272634 | -1.49557143 |
| Indiana | -2.17726883 | -1.21566195 | -0.67880001 | -1.42915840 | -1.74185735 |
| Kentucky | -2.31839936 | -1.26926054 | -0.69489994 | -1.49593905 | -1.83715998 |
| Louisiana | -1.60160305 | -0.99359914 | -0.61640776 | -1.13620002 | -1.33738726 |
| Maryland | 0.10161119 | 0.10709684 | 0.11287657 | 0.10527242 | 0.10341466 |
| Nebraska | 0.07022962 | 0.07261924 | 0.07506941 | 0.07194451 | 0.07107841 |
| Oklahoma | 0.49917358 | 0.70406163 | 0.99304011 | 0.62019695 | 0.55401828 |
| Oregon | -0.90510552 | -0.65451282 | -0.47330769 | -0.72189767 | -0.80517526 |

Looking at the deviance and Anscombe columns one is inclined to worry less about the effect of Texas as an outlier and more about Florida. This is because the Texas case has great influence on the parameter estimates and therefore the resulting $\mu_i$. Florida, for instance, is similar in many of the explanatory variable values to Texas but does not have nearly as many executions, and is subsequently further separated from the fit.

Pregibon (1981) suggests jackknifing out (temporarily removing for reanalysis) cases and looking at the resulting changes to the coefficient values. If the change is quite substantial, then we know that the jackknifed case had high influence on that coefficient. This can be done manually by removing the case and rerunning the analysis, but Pregibon also provides a one-step estimate (1981, p. 713) that is computationally superior for large data sets. Figure 6.1 is a modification of Pregibon's index plot construct in which all of the coefficients from the Poisson model of capital punishment are re-estimated jackknifing out the cases listed numerically on the $X$-axis by the order given in Table 4.2. The horizontal line indicates the coefficient value for the complete data matrix. Therefore, the distance between the point and the line indicates how much the coefficient estimate changes by removing this case.

Figure 6.1 shows that Texas does indeed exert great influence on the coefficient estimates. Index plots are an excellent way to show the effect of one or a few cases on the resulting estimates, but only for a relatively small number of cases. Picture Figure 6.1 with a sample size of several thousand. In these cases, one of several approaches are helpful. The researcher could sort the jackknifed values taking the top 5–10% in absolute value before plotting. These are the ones we are inclined to worry about anyway. Second, if interest was focused on an overall diagnostic picture rather than individual cases, the plot could show a smoothed function of the sorted index values rather than individual points as was done here.

## Measuring and Comparing Goodness of Fit

There are five primary methods for assessing how well a particular generalized linear model fits the data: the chi-square approximation to the Pearson statistic, the summed deviance, the Akaike information criterion, the Schwartz criterion, and graphical techniques. Each

62

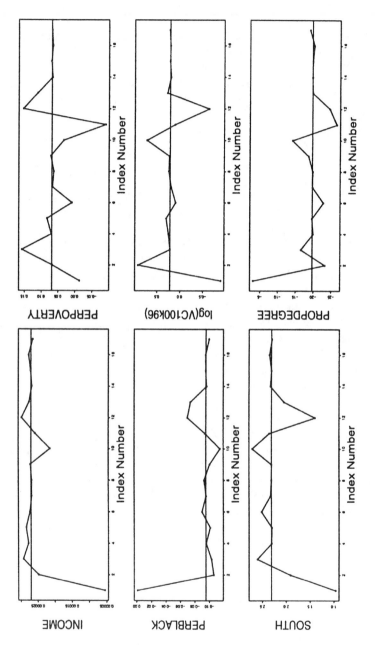

Figure 6.1. Jackknife Index Plot: Capital Punishment Model.

of these approaches is useful, but the summed deviance statistic appears to be the best overall measure of lack of fit because it provides the most intuitive indication of individual level contributions to the fit. However, no single measure provides "the right answer," and whenever possible more than one approach should be used.

The Pearson statistic is the sum of the squared Pearson residuals:

$$X^2 = \sum_{i=1}^{n} \mathbf{R}_{\text{Pearson}}^2 = \sum_{i=1}^{n} \left[ \frac{\mathbf{Y} - \boldsymbol{\mu}}{\sqrt{\text{VAR}[\boldsymbol{\mu}]}} \right]^2. \tag{6.4}$$

If the sample size is sufficiently large, then $X^2/a(\phi) \sim \chi_{n-k}^2$ where $n$ is the sample size and $k$ is the number of explanatory variables including the constant. Unfortunately, this statistic is very poorly behaved for relatively small sample sizes and readers should be wary of reported values based on double digit sample sizes (as in Example 4.2). The utility of this distributional property is that large $X^2$ values are determined to reside in the tail of the $\chi^2$ distribution and the model can therefore be "rejected" as poorly fitting.

The summed deviance has already been presented in this chapter, but not discussed as a measure of goodness of fit. Given sufficient sample size, it is also true that $D(\boldsymbol{\theta}, \mathbf{y})/a(\psi) \sim \chi_{n-k}^2$. However, for enumerative outcome data (dichotomous, counts), the convergence of the deviance function to a $\chi_{n-k}^2$ is much slower than the Pearson statistic. In any case involving enumerative data, one is strongly advised to add or subtract $\frac{1}{2}$ to each outcome variable in the direction of the mean. This continuity correction greatly improves the distributional result. Pierce and Schafer (1986) as well as Peers (1971) remind us, though, that just because the Pearson statistic is more nearly chi-square distributed, it does not mean that it is necessarily a superior measure of fit than the summed deviance. Although, the summed deviance is somewhat more problematic with regard to the discreteness of the outcome variables, it is vastly superior when considering likelihood-based inference.

A third, completely unexplored, alternative is to exploit the similarity between Anscombe residuals and deviance residuals, and create a new goodness of fit statistic that is simply the summed square of the Anscombe residuals. This has the advantage of being less ill-affected by enumerative outcome variables. The logic of this proposal is based on Pierce and Schafer's observation that "Whether one uses the deviance or Anscombe residuals is a matter of taste and computational convenience." (1986, p. 985).

Deviance residuals are also very useful for comparing to a proposed, nested model specification. In the previous discussion, the outer nesting model was the saturated model, but it need not be. Suppose we are comparing two nested model specifications, $M_1$ and $M_2$ with $p < n$ and $q < p$ parameters, respectively. Then the likelihood ratio statistic:

$$\frac{D(M_1) - D(M_2)}{a(\psi)}$$

is distributed approximately $\chi^2_{p-q}$ subject to a few complications (see Fahrmeir & Tutz, 1994; or McCullagh & Nelder, 1989). If we do not know the value of $a(\psi)$, such as in the Poisson case, then it is estimated and a modified likelihood ratio statistic is used:

$$\frac{D(M_1) - D(M_2)}{a(\hat{\psi})(p - q)}.$$

This modified statistic is distributed according to the $F$-distribution with $n - p$ and $p - q$ degrees of freedom.

A commonly used measure of goodness of fit is the Akaike information criterion (AIC) (Akaike, 1973, 1974, 1976). The principle is to select a model that minimizes the negative likelihood penalized by the number of parameters,

$$\text{AIC} = -2l(\hat{\theta}|\mathbf{y}) + 2p, \tag{6.5}$$

where $l(\hat{\theta}|\mathbf{y})$ is the maximized model log likelihood value and $p$ is the number of explanatory variables in the model (including the constant). This construct is very useful in comparing and selecting nonnested model specifications, but the practitioner should certainly not rely exclusively on AIC criteria. Many authors have noted that the AIC has a strong bias toward models that overfit with extra parameters since the penalty component is obviously linear with increases in the number of explanatory variables, and the log likelihood often increases more rapidly (Carlin & Louis, 1996, p. 49; Neftçi, 1982, p. 539; Sawa, 1978, p. 1280). However, a substantial benefit is that by including a penalty for increasing degrees of freedom, the AIC explicitly recognizes that basing model quality decisions on the value of the log likelihood alone is a poor strategy since the likelihood never decreases by adding more explanatory variables *regardless of their inferential quality.*

Another commonly used measure of goodness of fit is that proposed by Schwarz (1978), called both the Schwarz criterion and the Bayesian information criterion (BIC). Even though it is derived from a different statistical perspective, the BIC resembles the AIC in calculation,

$$\text{BIC} = -2l(\hat{\boldsymbol{\theta}}|\mathbf{y}) + p \log(n), \tag{6.6}$$

where $n$ is the sample size. Despite the strong visual similarity expressed between the AIC and the BIC, the two measures can indicate different model specifications from a set of alternatives as being optimal, with the AIC favoring more explanatory variables and a better fit and the BIC favoring fewer explanatory variables (parsimony) and a poorer fit (Koehler & Murphree, 1988, p. 188; Neftçi, 1982, p. 537; Sawa, 1978, p. 1280). Since the BIC explicitly includes sample size in the calculation, it is obviously more appropriate in model comparisons where sample size differs, and a model that can achieve a reasonable log likelihood fit with a smaller sample is penalized less than a comparable model with a larger sample. Whereas the AIC is just a convenient construction loosely derived from maximum likelihood and negative entropy (Amemiya, 1985, p. 147; Greene, 1997, p. 401; Koehler & Murphree, 1988, p. 189), the BIC is strongly connected with Bayesian theory. For instance, as $n \to \infty$,

$$\frac{(\text{BIC}_a - \text{BIC}_b) - \log B}{\log B} \to 0,$$

where $\text{BIC}_a$ and $\text{BIC}_b$ are the BIC quantities for competing model specifications $a$ and $b$, and $B$ is the Bayes factor between these models. Therefore, the BIC is an approximation to the log of the Bayes factor that is often much easier to calculate (Kass, 1993).

There are other competing model selection criteria as well as modifications of the AIC and the BIC that provide useful comparisons, but the basic Akaike and Schwarz constructs dominate empirical work. Although it can be shown that nearly all of these measures are asymptotically equivalent (Zhang, 1992), Amemiya (1980) provides simulation evidence that the BIC finds the correct model more often than the AIC for small samples. However, Neftçi's (1982) study found that the BIC was noticeably more sensitive to transformations on the data than the AIC. Since these measures are only one part of the assessment of model quality and neither has remarkably superior properties, the choice of which to use is primarily a function of personal preference. Amemiya states his preference for the AIC due to its simplicity (1981, p. 1505, footnote 13), and statistical software packages generally give the AIC as the default measure.

## Asymptotic Properties

It is convenient at this point to briefly review some asymptotic properties of the estimated quantities from a generalized linear model: coefficients, goodness of fit statistics, and residuals. The coefficients are maximum likelihood estimates generated by a numerical technique (iterative weighted least squares) rather than an analytical approach. This means that the extensive theoretical foundation developed for maximum likelihood estimation applies in this case, and this section reviews the conditions under which these principles hold. I also extend the discussion of the asymptotic chi-square distribution of the two primary test statistics, as well as review some large-$n$ properties of the residuals from a generalized linear model fit.

Chapter 5 introduced the Hessian matrix as the second derivative of the likelihood function at the maximum likelihood values, $\hat{\theta}$. The negative expectation of this matrix,

$$I(\theta) = -E_\theta \left( \frac{\partial^2}{\partial\theta \, \partial\theta^l} l(\theta^{(j)} | y) \right),$$

is called the *information matrix*, and plays an important role in evaluating the asymptotic behavior of the estimator. A useful and theoretically important feature of a given square matrix is the set of *eigenvalues* associated with this matrix. Every $p \times p$ matrix, $A$, has $p$ scalar values, $\lambda_i$, $i = 1, \ldots, p$, such that: $Ah_i = \lambda_i h_i$ for some corresponding vector, $h_i$. In this decomposition, $\lambda_i$ is called an eigenvalue of $A$ and $h_i$ is called an eigenvector of $A$. These eigenvalues show important structural features of the matrix. For instance, the number of nonzero eigenvalues is the rank of the $A$, the sum of the eigenvalues is the trace of $A$, and the product of the eigenvalues is the determinant of $A$.

The information matrix is especially easy to work with because it is symmetric, and unless there are serious computational problems, it is also positive definite. Generalized linear models built upon exponential families and natural link functions produce positive definite information matrices under very reasonable regularity conditions:

1. The sample space for the coefficient vector is open in $\Re^k$ and convex for $k$ explanatory variables,
2. the linear predictor transformed by the link function is defined over the sample space of the outcome variable,
3. the link function is twice differentiable,
4. the $X'X$ matrix is full rank.

These conditions are explored in much greater detail in Fahrmeir and Kaufman (1985), Lehmann and Casella (1988), and Le Cam and Yang (1990). Given the foregoing regularity conditions, if (1) small changes in the coefficient estimate produce arbitrarily small changes in the normed information matrix in any direction, and (2) the smallest absolute eigenvalue of the information matrix produces asymptotic divergence: $\lambda_{\min} I(\theta) \underset{n \to \infty}{\longrightarrow} \infty$, then the coefficient estimator: (1) exists, (2) converges in probability to the true value, and (3) is asymptotically normal with a covariance matrix equal to the inverse of the information matrix. This is summarized by the notation: $\sqrt{n}(\hat{\theta} - \theta) \overset{\mathscr{P}}{\to} n(0, I(\theta)^{-1})$. A condition of divergence seems odd at first, but recall that the information matrix functions in the denominator of expressions for variances. These conditions are only very broadly stated here and for details the reader should consult Fahrmeir and Tutz (1994, Appendix A2).

It has been shown that the maximum likelihood estimates from these models are still reasonably well behaved under more challenging circumstances than those required in the last paragraph. These applications include: clustered units (Bradley & Gart, 1962, Zeger & Karim, 1991), non-i.i.d. samples (Nordberg, 1980, Jørgensen, 1983), sparse tables (Brown & Fuchs, 1983), generalized autoregressive linear models (Kaufman, 1987), and mixed models (McGilchrist, 1994). It is easy to be relatively comfortable under typical or even these more challenging circumstances, provided there is a large sample size. Not having that luxury, what can be done to check asymptotic conditions?

The primary diagnostic advise is to check the minimum absolute eigenvalue from the information matrix, which can also be normalized prior to eigenanalysis to remove the scale of the explanatory variables. Some statistical packages make it relatively easy to evaluate this quantity (Splus, R, Gauss, LIMDEP). For any package that provides a variance–covariance matrix there is a handy shortcut. If $\lambda_i$ is an eigenvalue of the matrix $\mathbf{A}$, then $1/\lambda_i$ is an eigenvalue of the matrix $\mathbf{A}^{-1}$, provided it exists (nonsingular). So we can evaluate the inverse of the maximum eigenvalue of the variance–covariance matrix instead of the minimum eigenvalue of the information matrix.

It is desirable that $\lambda_{\min}$ not have a double digit negative exponent component, but since the quantity is scale-dependent it is often useful to first normalize the information matrix. When it is not convenient (or possible) to evaluate the eigenstructure of the information matrix, other symptoms may help. If at least one of the coefficients has an extremely large standard error, it may be an indication of a very small minimum eigenvalue. This is a handy but imperfect approach.

The asymptotic properties of two important test statistics, the summed deviance and the Pearson statistic, were discussed in the last section. Under ideal circumstances, both of these converge in distribution to $\chi^2_{n-k}$. Of the two, the Pearson statistic possesses a superior chi-square approximation because it is composed of more nearly normal terms which are then squared. Pierce and Schafer (1986) show a noticeable difference in the behavior of these two statistics for a binomial model with $n = 20$ and $m = 10$. The advice here is to never depend exclusively on the asymptotic convergence of these measures for any sample size smaller than this. However, it is often the case that the social science researcher is not in a position to choose the sample size, and it is still always worth the effort to calculate these values.

Checking the distributional properties of the residuals can be helpful in diagnostic situations. In addition to constructing test statistics, the residuals themselves often provide important information. While the residuals from a generalized linear model are not required to be asymptotically normal around zero, systematic patterns in the distribution can be an indication of misspecification or mismeasurement. By far, the best method of evaluating the distribution of residuals is by graphing them various ways. Different methods are presented in the following examples.

*Example 6.2: Poisson Generalized Linear Model of Capital Punishment, Continued.* Returning very briefly to the Poisson model of capital punishment in Table 5.1, we see that the deviance function of 18.212 on 10 degrees of freedom for the specified model provides a substantial improvement over the null deviance (calculated from a model explaining all systematic effects by the mean) of 136.573. A chi-square test of the summed deviance finds that it is not in the tail with a predefined alpha-level of 0.05, suggesting a reasonable overall fit. In general, a quick test of fit is looking to see whether the summed deviance is not substantially larger than the degrees of freedom. Now we apply the suggested idea of summing squared Anscombe residuals. The result from performing this operation on the Anscombe residuals in Table 6.3 is 18.482, which is very nearly the same value as the summed deviance.

*Example 6.3: Gamma Generalized Linear Model of Electoral Politics in Scotland, Continued.* Assessing the quality of fit for the Scottish elections model is a bit more subtle than the other examples because of the units of the outcome variable and the relatively low variability of the effects. In fact, if one was willing to live without any explanatory value, summarizing the outcome variable with a mean only produces an amazingly low null deviance of 0.536072. However, we *are* interested in producing models that explain outcome variable changes with regard to specific factors. In attempting to do so here, the model produces a summed deviance of 0.087389, a good *reduction* in proportion. In addition, the minimum eigenvalue of the information matrix is 0.7564709.

In the previous description of this model, it was argued that an interaction term between the variables for council tax and female unemployment claims was useful in describing outcome variable behavior. Some evidence supporting this claim was found in the 95% confidence interval for the coefficient being bounded away from zero. How it adds to the overall quality of the model becomes more apparent after performing an analysis of deviance. This is provided in Table 6.4 where the terms are sequentially entered into the model, and therefore the calculation of the summed deviance, with the interaction being last.

Unfortunately, this analysis of deviance is always order-dependent so the deviance residual contribution from adding a specified variable as reported is conditional on the previously added variables. Regardless of this attribute, we can evaluate whether or not the interaction term contributes reasonably to the fit. It is placed last in the order of analysis so that whatever conclusion we reach, the value of this term is conditional fully on the rest of the terms in the model. From looking at the second and fourth columns, we can see that the marginal

TABLE 6.4
Analysis of Deviance for the Scottish Vote Model

| | Individual Variable | | Summed Statistic | | | |
|---|---|---|---|---|---|---|
| | df | Deviance Residual | df | Residual Deviance | F Statistic | P(>F) |
| Null model | | | 31 | 0.53607 | | |
| Council tax | 1 | 0.23227 | 30 | 0.30380 | 64.8037 | 0.0000... |
| Female unemployment | 1 | 0.11949 | 29 | 0.18431 | 33.3394 | 0.0000... |
| Standardized mortality | 1 | 0.02746 | 28 | 0.15685 | 7.6625 | 0.0106 |
| Economically active | 1 | 0.02298 | 27 | 0.13387 | 6.4109 | 0.0183 |
| GDP | 1 | 0.00052 | 26 | 0.13335 | 0.1435 | 0.7081 |
| Percent aged 5–15 | 1 | 0.00732 | 25 | 0.12603 | 2.0438 | 0.1657 |
| Council tax: Female unemployment | 1 | 0.03864 | 24 | 0.08739 | 10.7806 | 0.0031 |

contribution from the interaction term is nontrivial. More importantly, we can test the hypothesis that the variable contributes to the fit of the model using the $F$ test previously described (since the dispersion parameter, $a(\psi)$, was estimated). For a model on row $k$ of the table with $p_k$ degrees of freedom nested within a model on row $k-1$ with $p_{k-1}$ degrees of freedom (necessarily larger), this test statistic is calculated:

$$f_{k, k-1} = \frac{D(M_{k-1}) - D(M_k)}{a(\hat{\psi})(p_{k-1} - p_k)}.$$

So the $F$ statistic on the last row of Table 6.4 is calculated by

$$f_{9, 8} = \frac{0.12603 - 0.08739}{(0.003584182)(25 - 24)} = 10.7806,$$

indicating strong evidence that the interaction term should be included in the model (note the $p$-value in the last column of Table 6.4). In addition, we can readily see corroborating evidence that GDP is not particularly reliable or important in the context of this model. Interestingly, the variable indicating the percentage of middle range children does not seem to be contributing a substantial amount to our summed deviance reduction, *even though it has a 95% confidence interval bounded away from zero.*

*Example 6.4: Binomial Generalized Linear Model of Educational Standardized Testing.* Measuring and modeling the educational process is a particularly difficult empirical task. Furthermore, we are typically not only interested in describing the current state of the educational institutions and policies; we seek to explain what policies "work" and why. Even defining whether or not a program is successful can be difficult and about the only principle that scholars in this area agree on is that our current understanding is rudimentary at best (Boyd, 1998).

There are two primary academic schools of thought on the problem. Economists (Hanushek, 1981, 1986, 1994; Boyd & Hartman, 1998; Becker & Baumol, 1996) generally focus on the parametric specification of the production function (a "systems" model of the process which evaluates outputs as a function of definable and measurable inputs). Conversely, education scholars (Hedges, Laine, & Greenwald, 1994; Wirt & Kirst, 1975) tend to evaluate more qualitatively, seeking macrotrends across cases and time as well as the implications of changing laws and policies. These two approaches often develop contradictory findings as evidenced by bitter debates such as in the determination of the marginal value of decreasing class size.

This example examines recent California state data on educational policy and outcomes (STAR program results for 1998). The data came from standardized testing by the California Department of Education (CDE) that required evaluation of 2nd–11th grade students by the Stanford 9 test on a variety of subjects. These data are recorded for individuals and aggregated at various levels from schools to the full state.[12] The level of analysis here is the unified school district, providing 303 cases. The outcome variable is the number of 9th graders scoring over the mathematics national median value for the district given the total number of 9th graders taking the mathematics exam (hence a binomial GLM).

The explanatory variables are grouped into two functional categories. The first, environmental factors, includes four variables traditionally used in the literature that are typically powerful explanations of learning outcomes. The proportion of low income students (LOWINC) is measured by the percentage of students who qualify for reduced or free lunch plans. Proportions of minority students are also included (PERASIAN, PERBLACK, and PERHISP). Poverty has been shown to strongly affect education outcomes. Racial variables are often important because according to numerous studies, economic factors and discrimination negatively and disproportionately affect particular minorities in terms of educational outcomes.

The second group, policy factors, includes six explanatory variables. These are: per-pupil expenditures in thousands of dollars (PER-SPEN), median teacher salary including benefits also in thousands of dollars (AVSAL), mean teacher experience in years (AVYRSEX), the pupil–teacher ratio in the classroom (PTRATIO), the percent of minority teachers (PERMINTE), the percent of students taking college credit courses (PCTAF), the percent of schools in the district which are charter schools (PCTCHRT), and the percent of schools in the district operating year-round programs (PCTYRRND).

The model is set up with a logit link function

$$g(\mu) = \log\left(\frac{\mu}{1 - \mu}\right),$$

although nearly identical results were observed with the probit and cloglog link functions. In addition to the listed variables, several interactions are added to the model. The outcome is listed in Table 6.5.

Each of the 20 included explanatory variables in the model produced a 95% confidence interval bounded away from zero (but not the intercept). Actually, if Table 6.5 were constructed with 99.9% intervals instead of 95%, then every interval would still be bounded away from zero. As expected, the environmental variables are reliable indicators of educational outcomes. Increasing the percent of minority teachers appears to improve learning outcomes. This is consistent with findings in the literature that suggest that minority students are greatly assisted by minority teachers while nonminority students are not correspondingly ill-affected (Meier, Stewart, & England, 1991; Murnane, 1975).

The large and negative coefficients for pupil–teacher ratios support current public policy efforts (particularly in California) to reduce class sizes. This, of course, comes with a cost. Since the coefficient is large and positive for the teachers' experience variable, bringing in many new and necessarily inexperienced teachers has at least a short run negative effect. Furthermore, the negative coefficient on the interaction effect between percent minority teachers and years experience implies that more experienced teachers tend to be nonminorities. So, the positive effect of hiring new minority teachers could be reduced slightly by their short-term inexperience.

TABLE 6.5
Modeling the Standardized Testing Results

| | Coefficient | Standard Error | 95% Confidence Interval |
|---|---|---|---|
| (Intercept) | 2.95888662 | 1.54654073 | [−0.07227751: 5.99005075] |
| LOWINC | −0.01681504 | 0.00043394 | [−0.01766554:−0.01596454] |
| PERASIAN | 0.00992547 | 0.00060135 | [ 0.00874685: 0.01110409] |
| PERBLACK | −0.01872422 | 0.00074353 | [−0.02018152:−0.01726693] |
| PERHISP | −0.01423856 | 0.00043385 | [−0.01508890:−0.01338822] |
| PERMINTE | 0.25448779 | 0.02994463 | [ 0.19579738: 0.31317819] |
| AVYRSEXP | 0.24069470 | 0.05713726 | [ 0.12870773: 0.35268167] |
| AVSAL | 0.00008041 | 0.00001392 | [ 0.00005312: 0.00010770] |
| PERSPEN | −0.00195217 | 0.00031677 | [−0.00257302:−0.00133131] |
| PTRATIO | −0.33408755 | 0.06125620 | [−0.45414750:−0.21402760] |
| PCTAF | −0.16902241 | 0.03269571 | [−0.23310482:−0.10494000] |
| PCTCHRT | 0.00491671 | 0.00125387 | [ 0.00245917: 0.00737425] |
| PCTYRRND | −0.00357997 | 0.00022546 | [−0.00402186:−0.00313807] |
| PERMINTE.AVYRSEXP | −0.01407660 | 0.00190451 | [−0.01780937:−0.01034383] |
| PERMINTE.AVSAL | −0.00000401 | 0.00000047 | [−0.00000493:−0.00000308] |
| AVYRSEXP.AVSAL | −0.00000391 | 0.00000096 | [−0.00000579:−0.00000202] |
| PERSPEN.PTRATIO | 0.00009171 | 0.00001451 | [ 0.00006328: 0.00012015] |
| PERSPEN.PCTAF | 0.00004899 | 0.00000745 | [ 0.00003439: 0.00006359] |
| PTRATIO.PCTAF | 0.00804075 | 0.00149924 | [ 0.00510228: 0.01097922] |
| PERMINTE.AVYRSEXP.AVSAL | 0.00000022 | 0.00000003 | [ 0.00000016: 0.00000028] |
| PERSPEN.PTRATIO.PCTAF | −0.00000225 | 0.00000035 | [−0.00000293:−0.00000157] |

Null deviance: 34,345, $df = 302$
Summed deviance: 4078.8, $df = 282$

Maximized $l()$: − 2999.6
AIC: 6039.2

Without a little background, the sign of the coefficient for percent of schools within the district operating year-round is perplexing. A common argument for year-round schools is that the relatively long time that students have away from the classroom in the summer means that part of the school year is spent catching up and remembering previous lessons. However, year-round schools come in two flavors: single track in which all of the students are on the same schedule, and multitrack in which the students share classrooms and other resources by alternating schedules. Evidence is that multitrack schools perform noticeably worse for various sociological reasons than single-track schools and traditionally scheduled schools (Weaver, 1992; Quinlan, 1987).

Often the best way to understand generalized linear models with interaction effects is by using first differences. The principle of first differences is to select two levels of interest for a given explanatory variable and to calculate the difference in impact on the outcome variable holding all of the other variables constant at some value, usually the mean. Therefore, when looking at a variable of interest in a table of first differences, the observed difference includes the main effect *as well as all of the interaction effects that include that particular variable*.

Table 6.6 provides first differences for each main effect variable in the two models over the interquartile range and over the whole range. Thus, for example, the interquartile range for percent low income is 26.68–55.46%, and the first difference for this explanatory variable over this interval is −11.89%. In other words, districts do about 12% worse at the third quartile than at the first quartile.

Looking at first differences clarifies some of the perplexing results from Table 6.5. For instance, the coefficient for per student spending in Table 6.5 has negative coefficient (−1.95217 using dollars as the measure). This is the contribution of this explanatory value in the nonsensical scenario where all other interacting variables are fixed at zero. If there is a large discrepancy between the magnitude of the effect in the estimation table and the first difference result, it means that the interactions dominate the zero-effect marginal. The first differences for per student spending in the model, moving from the first quartile to the third quartile improves the expected pass rate about 1% and moving across the whole range of spending for districts improves the expected pass rate slightly less than 6%.

TABLE 6.6
First Differences for the Standardized Testing Results Model

| Main Effect | Interquartile Range | | Full Range | |
|---|---|---|---|---|
| | Values | First Difference | Values | First Difference |
| **Percent low income** | [26.68:55.46] | −0.1189 | [ 0.00: 92.33] | −0.3620 |
| Percent Asian | [ 0.88: 7.19] | 0.0154 | [ 0.00: 63.20] | 0.1555 |
| **Percent Black** | [ 0.85: 5.96] | −0.0237 | [ 0.00: 76.88] | −0.2955 |
| **Percent Hispanic** | [13.92:47.62] | −0.1184 | [ 2.25: 98.82] | −0.3155 |
| **Percent minority teachers** | [ 6.33:19.18] | 0.0144 | [ 0.00: 80.17] | 0.0907 |
| Average years experience | [13.03:15.51] | −0.0024 | [ 8.42: 20.55] | −0.0117 |
| Average salary | [55.32:62.21] | 0.0210 | [39.73: 80.57] | 0.1243 |
| **Per-pupil spending** | [ 3.94: 4.51] | 0.0080 | [ 2.91: 6.91] | 0.0559 |
| Class size | [21.15:24.12] | 0.0042 | [14.32: 28.21] | 0.0197 |
| Percent in college courses | [23.45:41.80] | 0.0224 | [ 0.00: 89.13] | 0.1093 |
| Percent charter | [ 0.00: 0.00] | 0.0000 | [ 0.00: 71.43] | 0.0875 |
| Percent year-around | [ 0.00:12.31] | −0.0109 | [ 0.00:100.00] | −0.0863 |

**Bold** coefficient names denote 95% CI bounded away from zero

Of great concern is the summed deviance of 4078.8 on 282 degrees of freedom (4054.928 for adjusted deviances). Clearly, this is in the tail of the chi-square distribution (no formal test needed) and none of the smoothing techniques in the literature will have an effect. First it should be noted that the deviance was reduced about 90% from the null. This observation along with the high quality of the coefficient estimates and the minimum eigenvalue (0.4173) of the information matrix, motivate further investigation as to whether the fit is acceptable.

Figure 6.2 provides three very useful diagnostics for looking at the quality of the fit for the developed model. The first panel provides a comparison of the fitted values, $g^{-1}(\mathbf{X\beta})$, versus the observed outcome variable values, $\mathbf{Y}$. The diagonal line in this panel is the linear regression line of the fitted values regressed on these observed values. If this were the saturated model, then all of the points would land on the line. So a model's difference from the saturated benchmark is the degree to which the points deviate from the line. If there existed systematic bias in the fit, say from omitted variables, then the slope would be much different than one. For instance, a slope noticeably less than one would indicate that the model systematically *underfit* cases with larger observed values and *overfit* cases with smaller oberved values. In Figure 6.2, the linear regression produces an intercept and a slope ($\alpha = -0.004961283$ and $\beta = 0.989823091$) which are very near the perfect ideal.

Panel two in Figure 6.2 displays a residual dependence plot. These are the fitted values, $g^{-1}(\mathbf{X}_i \hat{\boldsymbol{\beta}})$, plotted against the Pearson residuals. Any discernible pattern or curvature in a residual dependence plot is an indication of either: systematic effects contained within the stochastic term, a poor choice for the link function, or a very badly measured variable. This plot shows a very healthy residuals structure.

The final panel in Figure 6.2 plots the deviance residual quantiles ($Y$-axis) against the quantiles from an equal number of sorted normal variates with mean zero and standard deviation one. The purpose of this normal-quantile plot is to evaluate whether or not the obtained deviance residuals are approximately normally distributed. If one were to plot perfectly normally distributed residuals against the $N(0, 1)$ benchmark here, the plot would be an approximately straight line with slope equal to the mean of the normal variates.

For the model developed here, there is evidence that the deviance residuals are approximately normally distributed. Again, we can see

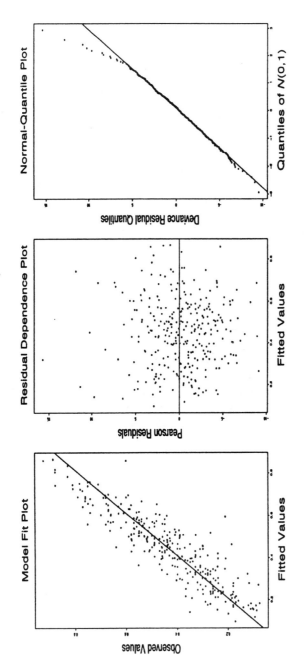

Figure 6.2. Diagnostics: Education Policy Model.

some outliers at the end, but these are small in number and not terribly ill-behaved. Indications of residual distributions that deviate strongly from the desired normality show up as "S" type curves in the normal-quantile plot. It should be noted again that generalized linear models are not required to have normally distributed residuals. Therefore, linearity in the normal-quantile plot in this context is not a *condition* of model quality, rather a helpful description of residuals behavior.

This residuals analysis shows that it is unlikely that the model suffers from omitted variable bias affecting the stochastic component or misspecification of the link function. The summed deviance could probably be reduced significantly by including an explanatory variable that many researchers have pointed to as a critical determinant in the education production function: parental involvement, possibly measured by the level of PTA activity. Unfortunately, the State of California does not track and measure this variable for these data.

*Example 6.5: Negative Binomial Generalized Linear Model, Congressional Activity: 1995.* As a simple illustration of one use for a negative binomial GLM, consider the assignment of bills to committees during the first 100 days that the House of Representatives is in session after an election. This period is typically quite busy as Congress usually sees election issues as subsequent legislative mandates (though not always with successful or intended successful outcomes). The first 100 days of the 104th House was certainly no exception to this observed phenomenon. The new Republican majority busily addressed 40 years of minority party frustration and attempted to fulfill their promises outlined in the "Contract with America."

The negative binomial distribution has the same sample space (i.e., on the counting measure) as the Poisson, but contains an additional parameter which can be thought of as gamma distributed and therefore used to model a variance function. This configuration, Poisson distributed mean and gamma distributed variance, naturally produces the negative binomial PMF. In this manner, we can model counts while relaxing the assumption that the mean and variance are identical. This turns out to be enormously useful for count data that is observed to be overdispersed: $VAR[Y] = \delta E[Y]$, $\delta \gg 1$. Often when there is noticeable heterogeneity in the sample, such overdispersion results.

The data in this example contain the number of bills assigned to committee in the first 100 days of the 103rd and 104th Houses, the number of members on the committee, the number of subcommittees, the number of staff assigned to the committee, and a dummy variable indicating whether or not it is a high prestige committee. These data are provided in Table 6.7.

If bill assignments in the 104th House are perceived as events (at the committee level), then it is natural to consider applying a generalized linear model with a Poisson link function. Unfortunately, this model fits poorly as measured by some of the diagnostics already discussed (summed deviance of 393.43 on 14 degrees of freedom, for example). The culprit appears to be a variance term that is larger than the expected value, and thus violates a Poisson assumption, motivating the negative binomial specification developed here.

The negative binomial model is developed with the link function: $\theta = \log(1 - \mu)$. It is possible with many statistical packages to either assign a known value for the variance function or to estimate it. Given that we have no prior information about the nature of the variance function, it is estimated here. The resulting output is provided in Table 6.8.

From Table 6.8, we can see that the model provides a quite reasonable fit. The summed deviance term is not in the tail of a chi-square distribution for 13 degrees of freedom, and the smallest eigenvalue of the information matrix is 0.1366226. The dispersion parameter is estimated to be $a(\phi) = 1.494362$, indicating that we were justified in developing a negative binomial specification for these counts.

Both the coefficients for the prestige variable and the variable for the size of the committee (measured by number of members) have 95% confidence intervals that bound zero. There is therefore no evidence that these are important determinants of the quantity of bills assigned, given these data and this formulated model. This is interesting because some committees in Congress are larger presumably because they have more activity. However, the size of the committee is likely to be affected by 40 years of Democratic policy priorities as well. Other measures of size and resources for a committee is its number of staff and its subcommittees. The corresponding coefficients for both of these both have 95% confidence intervals bounded away from zero. Predictably, the interaction term for these variables also has a 95% confidence interval bounded away from zero, although the negative sign is mysterious.

TABLE 6.7
Bills Assigned to Committee, First 100 Days

| Committee | Size | Subcommittees | Staff | Prestige | Bills—103rd | Bills—104th |
|---|---|---|---|---|---|---|
| Appropriations | 58 | 13 | 109 | 1 | 9 | 6 |
| Budget | 42 | 0 | 39 | 1 | 101 | 23 |
| Rules | 13 | 2 | 25 | 1 | 54 | 44 |
| Ways and Means | 39 | 5 | 23 | 1 | 542 | 355 |
| Banking | 51 | 5 | 61 | 0 | 101 | 125 |
| Economic-Educational Opportunities | 43 | 5 | 69 | 0 | 158 | 131 |
| Commerce | 49 | 4 | 79 | 0 | 196 | 271 |
| International Relations | 44 | 3 | 68 | 0 | 40 | 63 |
| Government Reform | 51 | 7 | 99 | 0 | 72 | 149 |
| Judiciary | 35 | 5 | 56 | 0 | 168 | 253 |
| Agriculture | 49 | 5 | 46 | 0 | 60 | 81 |
| National security | 55 | 7 | 48 | 0 | 75 | 89 |
| Resources | 44 | 5 | 58 | 0 | 98 | 142 |
| Transportation-Infrastructure | 61 | 6 | 74 | 0 | 69 | 155 |
| Science | 50 | 4 | 58 | 0 | 25 | 27 |
| Small Business | 43 | 4 | 29 | 0 | 9 | 8 |
| Veterans Affairs | 33 | 3 | 36 | 0 | 41 | 28 |
| House Oversight | 12 | 0 | 24 | 0 | 233 | 68 |
| Standards of Conduct | 10 | 0 | 9 | 0 | 0 | 1 |
| Intelligence | 16 | 2 | 24 | 0 | 2 | 4 |

Source: Congressional Index, Congessional Register

TABLE 6.8
Modeling Bill Assignment—104th House, First 100 Days

| | Coefficient | Standard Error | 95% Confidence Interval |
|---|---|---|---|
| (Intercept) | −6.80543 | 2.54651 | [−12.30683:−1.30402] |
| Size | −0.02825 | 0.02093 | [ − 0.07345: 0.01696] |
| Subcommittees | 1.30159 | 0.54370 | [ 0.12701: 2.47619] |
| log(Staff) | 3.00971 | 0.79450 | [ 1.29329: 4.72613] |
| Prestige | −0.32367 | 0.44102 | [ − 1.27644: 0.62911] |
| Bills in 103rd | 0.00656 | 0.00139 | [ 0.00355: 0.00957] |
| Subcommittees: log(STAFF) | −0.32364 | 0.12489 | [ − 0.59345:−0.05384] |
| Null deviance: 107.314, $df = 19$ | | | Maximized $l(\ )$:10,559 |
| Summed deviance: 20.948, $df = 13$ | | | AIC: 121,130 |

It is not surprising that the coefficient for the variable indicating committee counts in the 103rd House is also reliable. Seemingly this tells us that party control and a change of agenda do not make huge changes in the assignment of bills to committee during the first 100 days of a Congress. In other words, a certain amount of work of a similar nature needs to take place regardless of policy priorities of the leadership.

Figure 6.3 shows another way of looking at model residuals. In this display, the Pearson residuals are shown by the dots and the deviance residuals are indicated by the length of the vertical lines. These residual quantities are both sorted by the order of the outcome variable. Therefore, if there were some unintended systematic effects in the stochastic term, we would expect to see some sort of a trend in the display. It is clear that none is present. The horizontal bands indicate one and two times the standard error of the Pearson residuals in both the positive and negative directions, and can be used to look for outlying points.

*Example 6.6: Two-Stage Generalized Linear Model, the World Copper Market: 1951–1975.* A common managerial economic problem is the estimation of a model of supply and demand functions for a certain good given data. A typical application is a linear regression model to find explanatory effects that influence market price and quantity

82

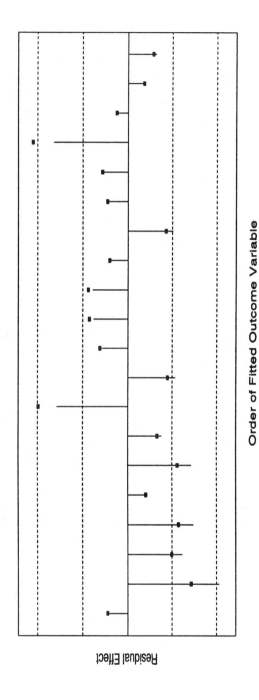

Figure 6.3. Residual Diagnostics: Bill Assignment Model.

from which elasticities can be calculated at selected points. The central problem is one of endogeneity: price affects demand and demand affects price. The classic solution is to implement a two-stage process in which the endogenous variable for price is regressed onto some exogenous variables to create a predicted price vector, then this predicted price vector is used as one of a set of explanatory variables to regress quantity. The model is fully identified if the first stage of the model has one or more explanatory variables not included in the second stage. If the regression technique used in this process is the standard linear model, then this is called two-stage least squares (2SLS).

This two-stage estimation process can be applied to the generalized linear model. The process performed here simply inserts a nonidentity link function at the regression stages. As an example, consider a model for the world demand for copper over the years 1951–1975. Maurice and Smithson (1985) provide a 2SLS model using: world consumption of copper in 1000 metric tons (QTY), the constant dollar adjusted price of copper (PRI), and aluminum (ALM, which is a substitute in many industrial settings), an index of real per capita income base 1970 (INC), and an annual measure of manufacturer inventory change (INV). As an attempt to capture technological improvements in manufacturing over this period, the authors use a simple integer time index 1–25 (TME) over the years as an additional explanatory variable. These data are provided in Table 6.9.

The first model provides predicted price of copper as a function of real income, the price of aluminum, inventories of copper, and the time surrogate for technological change. The second model gives the expected quantity produced as a function of the predicted price, real income, and the price of aluminum. The model is identified because time and inventories are excluded from the second stage. The 2SLS model can be summarized as

$$\text{Stage 1: Predicted(PRI)} = 1\beta_{10} + \text{INC }\beta_{11} + \text{ALM }\beta_{12}$$
$$+ \text{INV }\beta_{13} + \text{TME }\beta_{14}$$
$$\text{Stage 2: } E[\text{QTY}] = 1\beta_{20} + \text{Predicted(PRI) }\beta_{21}$$
$$+ \text{INC }\beta_{22} + \text{ALM }\beta_{23}.$$

From this specification Maurice and Smithson get a useful linear model for estimating the demand function conditioned on these

84

TABLE 6.9
The World Copper Market: 1951–1975

| Year | World Copper Consumption | Copper Price | Aluminum Price | Income Index | Inventory Change |
|------|--------------------------|--------------|----------------|--------------|------------------|
| 1951 | 3173.00 | 26.56 | 19.76 | 0.70 | 0.97679 |
| 1952 | 3281.10 | 27.31 | 20.78 | 0.71 | 1.03937 |
| 1953 | 3135.70 | 32.95 | 22.55 | 0.72 | 1.05153 |
| 1954 | 3359.10 | 33.90 | 23.06 | 0.70 | 0.97312 |
| 1955 | 3755.10 | 42.70 | 24.93 | 0.74 | 1.02349 |
| 1956 | 3875.90 | 46.11 | 26.50 | 0.74 | 1.04135 |
| 1957 | 3905.70 | 31.70 | 27.24 | 0.74 | 0.97686 |
| 1958 | 3957.60 | 27.23 | 26.21 | 0.72 | 0.98069 |
| 1959 | 4279.10 | 32.89 | 26.09 | 0.75 | 1.02888 |
| 1960 | 4627.90 | 33.78 | 27.40 | 0.77 | 1.03392 |
| 1961 | 4910.20 | 31.66 | 26.94 | 0.76 | 0.97922 |
| 1962 | 4908.40 | 32.28 | 25.18 | 0.79 | 0.99679 |
| 1963 | 5327.90 | 32.38 | 23.94 | 0.83 | 0.96630 |
| 1964 | 5878.40 | 33.75 | 25.07 | 0.85 | 1.02915 |
| 1965 | 6075.20 | 36.25 | 25.37 | 0.89 | 1.07950 |
| 1966 | 6312.70 | 36.24 | 24.55 | 0.93 | 1.05073 |
| 1967 | 6056.80 | 38.23 | 24.98 | 0.95 | 1.02788 |
| 1968 | 6375.90 | 40.83 | 24.96 | 0.99 | 1.02799 |
| 1969 | 6974.30 | 44.62 | 25.52 | 1.00 | 0.99151 |
| 1970 | 7101.60 | 52.27 | 26.01 | 1.00 | 1.00191 |
| 1971 | 7071.70 | 45.16 | 25.46 | 1.02 | 0.95644 |
| 1972 | 7754.80 | 42.50 | 22.17 | 1.07 | 0.96947 |
| 1973 | 8480.30 | 43.70 | 18.56 | 1.12 | 0.98220 |
| 1974 | 8105.20 | 47.88 | 21.32 | 1.10 | 1.00793 |
| 1975 | 7157.20 | 36.33 | 22.75 | 1.07 | 0.93810 |
| TME | QTY | PRI | INC | ALM | INV |

Source: Maurice and Smithson (1985).

exogenous variables. There is, however, a problem with the time variable as a measurement of technological improvement and change in the manufacturing process. There is evidence that this is not a linear change over these years, and in particular that most innovations occurred early in the time period. Using an integer scale as the 2SLS model has done, imposes a strict linearity condition here. An obvious fix is to drop the time-technology variable entirely, or to transform it in some logical manner. Unfortunately, these strategies produce a substantially worse fit to these data using the standard linear model.

A histogram of the outcome variable indicates a strongly right-skewed distribution, suggesting that the linear model might not be the best choice. In addition, there is a slight downturn for the last production value, indicating a discontinuation of the linear trend. Instead of the two-stage least squares linear model, a two-stage gamma GLM with $\theta = -1/\mu$ is built with the following specification:

$$\text{Stage 1: Predicted(PRI)} = g^{-1}[1\beta_{10} + \text{INC}\,\beta_{11} + \text{ALM}\,\beta_{12}$$
$$+ \text{INV}\,\beta_{13} + \log(\text{TME})\,\beta_{14}]$$
$$\text{Stage 2: } E[\text{QTY}] = g^{-1}[1\beta_{20} + \text{Predicted(PRI)}\,\beta_{21}$$
$$+ \text{INC}\,\beta_{22} + \text{ALM}\,\beta_{23}],$$

where the $g^{-1}(\mathbf{X}\boldsymbol{\beta})$ is the gamma link function. This model specification produces the results in Table 6.10.

Every term in the model produces a 95% confidence interval bounded away from zero. The summed deviance is far from being in the tail of the chi-square distribution for 21 degrees of freedom. The minimum of the eigenvalue of the normed information matrix is: $-0.0015$. By all accounts this model appears to fit these data quite well. While we should feel relatively satisfied with this model, it is still wise to look at some diagnostics such as the behavior of the residuals. Figure 6.4 gives these. There is little indication of a poor fit or of systematic effects remaining in the residuals.

Initially, the sign on the coefficient for price is surprising since a positive value implies that higher prices are associated with greater demand that contradicts basic theory for a normal good (the 2SLS

TABLE 6.10
Modeling the World Copper Market: 1951–1975

|  | Coefficient | Standard Error | 95% Confidence Interval |
|---|---|---|---|
| (Intercept) | 0.00080558 | 0.00006566 | [ 0.00066904: 0.00094212] |
| Predicted(PRI) | 0.00000449 | 0.00000162 | [ 0.00000111: 0.00000786] |
| INC | −0.00058689 | 0.00006905 | [−0.00073049:−0.00044329] |
| ALM | −0.00001082 | 0.00000234 | [−0.00001568:−0.00000596] |

| | |
|---|---|
| Null deviance: 2.36735, $df = 24$ | Maximized $l(\ )$ : $-185.755$ |
| Summed deviance: 0.14290, $df = 21$ | AIC: 379.51 |

86

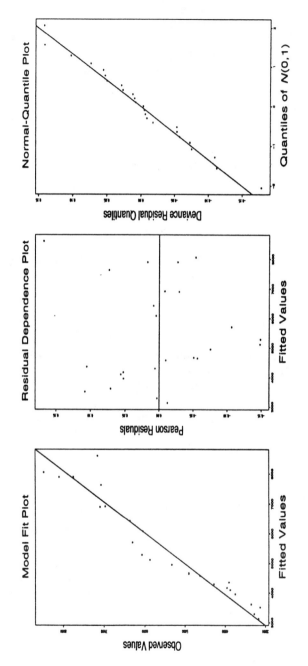

Figure 6.4. Diagnostics: World Copper Market Model.

model had a negative sign). However, once we recall that the link function is necessarily acting on the linear predictor, this makes sense. For example, we can construct the first difference for price using its first and third quartile (thus bracketing the interquartile range), keeping the other two variables constant at their mean. This produces: $E[\text{QTY}_{Q1}] = 5566.772$, and $E[\text{QTY}_{Q3}] = 4527.485$, for a first difference of $-1039.287$. So as price moves from the 25th percentile to the 75th percentile, the expected drop in the world for demand is a little over one million (1,039,287) metric tons.

## 7. CONCLUSION

### Summary

We started in Chapter 1 with a general introduction to the language and setup of generalized linear models. This was followed by some classic mathematical statistics theory in Chapter 2. Here we saw that most commonly used PDFs and PMFs can be expressed in a single exponential family form. This has the advantage of identifying and highlighting particular structural components such as $b(\theta)$ and $a(\psi)$. Likelihood theory and moment calculations using the exponential family form were provided in detail in Chapter 3. This material is important enough to fill volumes on its own (and in fact does so). Here we focused on calculating the first two moments and identifying the variance function. The most important chapter in the monograph followed. Chapter 4 provided the link from the standard linear setup, with interval measurement and assumed normality, to the broader class of outcome variable forms. The link function represents the core of generalized linear model theory since it is the mechanism that allows generalization beyond the Gauss–Markov assumptions. Chapter 5 discussed the important statistical computing issues associated with producing estimates for the generalized linear model. The basics of iterative weighted least squares was explained and demonstrated with examples. Chapter 6 contains the material that readers of generalized linear models care about most: does the prescribed model provide a good fit to the data? Here we looked at residuals analysis as well as some commonly applied tests.

Throughout the second half of the monograph, there has been an emphasis on looking at data. Except for the educational testing problem ($n = 303$), every example provided the raw data, and all examples included graphical displays to highlight various features of the data or model. The maxim that researchers should spend some time looking at the data before applying various parameterizations and summaries cannot be overemphasized. Furthermore, these examples are real, original data-analytic problems, not simply contrivances for presentational convenience. It is not infrequently the case that a text explains some data analytic procedure with the aid of a stylized simple "data set" that bears little resemblance to problems readers subsequently face in their own work. This disconnect can be very frustrating when applying principles in practice. However, since the data included here address actual, unpublished problems, they are necessarily more "messy," containing issues such as: a dominant outlier, small outcome variation, reliable coefficients but large deviance, and the need for a two-stage process. This is an intentional feature of the monograph as it better reflects the actual process of social science data analysis.

**Related Topics**

There are several associated and related topics not discussed in this monograph. An important application of generalized linear models is to the analysis of grouped and tabular data. Generalized linear models are quite adept at addressing these problems and the concerned reader is directed to Fahrmeir and Tutz (1994) or Lindsey (1997). Generalized additive models are a natural extension of a generalized linear model in which the form of the relationship between each explanatory variable and the outcome variable can be defined nonparametrically. This is a marvelously flexible tool despite some of the complications that can arise. However, even a well-developed generalized additive model lacks something that a generalized linear model necessarily possesses: a direct analytical expression for the model relationship. The seminal work on generalized additive models is Hastie and Tibshirani (1990).

**Further Reading**

The standard and classic reference for generalized linear models is McCullagh and Nelder (1989). Despite the popularity of this text, it remains somewhat elusive to many social scientists due to the level of discussion and the preponderance of biostatistics examples (lizards, beetles, wheezing coalminers, etc.). The article by Nelder and Wedderburn (1972) is well worth reading as it is the original defining work on generalized linear models. The recent book by Lindsey provides a wealth of extensions such as spatial interaction, dynamic modeling, and polynomial specifications. The advanced level book by Fahrmeir and Tutz (1994) is extremely rich in theory and offers many useful practical points to those with some experience in mathematical statistics. Dobson (1990) offers an accessible introduction with some useful problem sets.

Generalized linear models are also an active research area in the current statistics literature, and many extensions and refinements are being developed. Zeger and Karim (1991) apply generalized linear modeling to clustered data and use the Gibbs sampler to circumvent the ensuing intractable likelihood function. Others such as Su and Wei (1991) look extensively at assessing model quality in a variety of more complex settings. A generalized linear *mixed* model can be developed to accommodate outcome variables conditional on mixtures of possibly correlated random and fixed effects (Breslow & Clayton, 1993; Wang, Lin, Gutierrez, & Carroll, 1998; Wolfinger & O'Connell, 1993), but not without some computational challenges (McCulloch, 1997). Buonaccorsi (1996) develops tools for compensating for bias-inducing measurement error in the outcome variable.

As mentioned previously, quasi-likelihood functions are being applied to models that lift the restriction to exponential family forms. In this construct, only separate characterizations of the first two moments are required rather than a specific PDF or PMF. This literature begins roughly with Wedderburn (1974) and McCullagh (1983), but gains momentum with Chapter 9 of McCullagh and Nelder (1989). Some other works on quasi-likelihood generalized linear models have focused on a broader approach to modeling dispersion (Efron, 1986; Nelder & Pregibon, 1987; Pregibon, 1984).

The standard algorithm for computing parameter values, iterative weighted least squares (IWLS), is restricted at present to the exponential family form. Loosening this restriction is currently an active area of research. Härdle, Mammen, and Müller (1998) develop a generalized *partially* linear model and use Severini and Staniswalis' (1994) quasi-likelihood estimation algorithm. Generalized estimating equations (Liang & Zeger, 1986; Zeger & Liang, 1986) are an extension of generalized linear models that accommodate time series, or clustered research designs by allowing for autocorrelation although still requiring single-period independence. This approach (GEE) does not require that the functional form be identified as an exponential family form, yet it uses the same mean and variance function developed for generalized linear models for computational ease.

Bayesian variants of the generalized linear model have been used to incorporate prior information about the $\beta$ vector. The recent explosion in computing power available to researchers has tremendously benefited Bayesian approaches, some of which build upon the generalized linear model. Cook and Broemeling (1994), Albert (1988), and Naylor and Smith (1982) provide excellent overviews with an emphasis on computing issues. Other provocative works include Ibrahim and Laud (1991) on the use of a Jeffreys' prior, Walker and Mallick (1997) on frailty models, Zellner and Rossi (1984) on binary outcome variables, and West, Harrison, and Migon (1985) on forecasting. Hierarchical generalized linear models with Bayesian priors and hyperpriors are currently the vanguard in applied methods in this area. Good examples include Daniels and Gatsonis (1999), Albert and Chib (1996), Ghosh, Natarajan, Stroud, and Carlin (1998), as well as Bennet, Racine-Poon, and Wakefield (1996).

**Motivation**

The process of generating social science statistical models has four steps: obtaining and coding the data, specifying a probability model, applying the model to the data to obtain inferences, and finally determining the quality of the fit of the model to the data. This monograph directly addresses the last three steps with a unified process for developing and testing empirical models. Once a researcher is comfortable with the theoretical basis of the generalized linear model, then specification is simplified to two primary tasks: variable inclusion decisions and selection of an appropriate link function. In other words, it is not necessary to rattle through an extensive toolbox full of distinct and separate techniques.

The generalized linear model is a flexible, unified framework for applying parametric models to social science data. The flexibility stems from the broad class of probability statements that are included under the exponential family form. The theory bridges the chasm between discrete and continuous probability models by recasting both PDFs and PMFs into this common exponential family form. Therefore, provided that an appropriate link function is selected, the distinction between levels of measurement is not an important consideration.

The GLM framework includes an integrated set of techniques for evaluating and presenting goodness of fit for the specified model. By concentrating quality assessment on a more general measure, deviances, generalized linear models provide a more cohesive framework for gauging model quality. Furthermore, this approach moves attention away from flawed measures of model fit such as the $R^2$ measure in the linear model, common fixation with $p$-values, and linear misinterpretation of logit–probit coefficients.

Given that nearly every statistical computing software package readily accommodates the generalized linear modeling approach, there are few technical impediments to widespread use. The major impediment to widespread use is not technical, rather it is a reluctance to embrace the theory. The theoretical underpinnings can be somewhat challenging, and in particular when explained to a different audience. This monograph has taken the approach that understanding the theory is critical, but that it should be explained and applied in a way that social scientists find accessible.

# NOTES

1. For instance, suppose we had $V$ explanatory variables, where we can pick $r \leq V$ to include in a simple additive model. Then the total number of specifications is: $\sum_{r=1}^{V} \binom{V}{r}$. To illustrate, $V = 20$ produces $\sum_{r=1}^{20} \binom{20}{r} = 1,048,575$ possible models.

2. There are two notable exceptions. First, the interaction term in the saturated log-linear model for a contingency table (saturated in this context means that there are as many parameters as cells in the table) demonstrates the strength of association of a hypothesized relationship, and can be tested to provide inferential evidence of nonindependence. Useful discussions can be found in Bishop, Fienberg, and Holland (1975); Good (1986); Krzanowski (1988, Chap. 10); and Upton (1991). The second useful application of the saturated model is in a time series where there exists a time-varying parameter and it is desired to have an estimate for each point. In this setup, the parameters can be allowed to vary as smooth functions of the other variables and as a function of time (Harvey, 1989; Harvey & Koopman, 1993; Hastie & Tibshirani, 1993). These structural time series models are formulated to use unobserved features of the data that affect patterns of interest such as periodicity.

3. While this is strictly true, recent work has relaxed this assumption applying a wider class of probability functions in which full specification of the parametric form is replaced by merely characterizing the first two moments. This allows separating of the mean and variance functions and estimation is accomplished by employing a "quasilikelihood" function. This approach has the advantage of accommodating situations in which the data are not i.i.d. See Wedderburn (1974) and McCullagh (1983) for discussions.

4. It should be noted that most statistical packages do not allow an explicit form for the binomial coefficient or "choose" operator,

$$\binom{n}{y} = \frac{n!}{y!(n-y)!},$$

in an estimation routine. This is not a serious problem as the gamma function can be substituted according to

$$\binom{n}{y} = \frac{\Gamma(n+1)}{\Gamma(y+1)\Gamma(n-y+1)},$$

where $\Gamma(a) = \int_0^\infty t^{a-1} e^{-t} dt$.

5. An alternative but equivalent form,

$$f(y|r, p) = \binom{y-1}{r-1} p^r (1-p)^{y-r},$$

measures the number of trials necessary to get $r$ successes.

6. Specifically that one can apply Leibnitz's rule for constant bounds $(a, b)$: $d/d\psi \int_a^b f(y, \psi) \, dy = \int_a^b (\partial/\partial\psi) f(y, \psi) \, dy$, or Lebesgue's dominated convergence theorem for infinite bounds: $d/d\psi \int_{-\infty}^\infty f(y, \psi) \, dy = \int_{\infty}^\infty (\partial/\partial\psi) f(y, \psi) \, dy$ where there exists some function $g(y) \geq |(f(y, \psi)|$ such that $\int_{-\infty}^\infty g(y) < \infty$.

7. For discrete random variables, replace the integration with the summation in (3.5).

8. This measure includes AA degree and above. The observed figures appear low since children and currently enrolled college students are included in the denominator. It also does not count college attendance short of receiving a degree.

9. For an example see "WORKSHOP: A Unified Theory of Generalized Linear Models," Jeff Gill, presented to the Boston Chapter of the American Statistical Association, February, 1998. Available at: http://web.clas.ufl.edu/~jgill.

10. A matrix, $\mathbf{A}$, is positive definite if for any nonzero $k \times 1$ vector $\mathbf{x}$, $\mathbf{x'Ax} > 0$.

11. I have reproduced this mathematical function for $a - 1 = -1/3$, $b - 1 = -1/3$ and was able to exactly replicate Cox and Snell's table using Laguerre–Gaussian quadrature. This table and lookup routines written for various statistical packages is available in electronic form at my webpage: http://web.clas.ufl.edu/~jgill. The provided form of the Cox and Snell table is changed from the original in that it is now two column vectors: the first is the index value and the second is the $I(\ )$ value. This approach facilitates software lookup rather than the traditional Fisheresque approach with column and row indices requiring human interaction. A partial reason that Anscombe residuals are less popular than other forms is the difficulty in obtaining these tabular values.

12. The data sets are freely available from the source (http://goldmine.cde.ca.gov) or my webpage. Demographic data are provided by CDE's educational demographics unit, and income data are provided by the National Center for Education Statistics. For some nontrivial data collection and aggregation issues see Theobald and Gill (1999).

## REFERENCES

AKAIKE, H. (1973). Information theory and an extension of the maximum likelihood principle. In N. Petrov & Csàdki (Eds.), *Proceedings of the Second International Symposium on Information Theory* (pp. 716–723). Budapest: Akadémiai Kiadó.

AKAIKE, H. (1974). A new look at statistical model identification. *IEEE Transactions on Automatic Control, AU-19*, 716–722.

AKAIKE, H. (1976). Canonical correlation analysis of time series and the use of an information criterion. In R. K. Mehra & D. G. Lainiotis (Eds.), *System identification: Advances and case studies*, (pp. 52–107). New York: Academic Press.

ALBERT, J. H. (1988). Computational methods using a Bayesian hierarchical generalized linear model. *Journal of the American Statistical Association, 83*, 1037–1044.

ALBERT, J. H., & Chib, S. (1996). Bayesian tests and model diagnostics in conditionally independent hierarchical models. *Journal of the American Statistical Association, 92*, 916–925.

AMEMIYA, T. (1980). Selection of regressors. *International Economic Review, 21*, 331–354.

AMEMIYA, T. (1981). Qualitative response models: A survey. *Journal of Economic Literature, XIX*, 1483–1536.

AMEMIYA, T. (1985). *Advanced econometrics*. Cambridge, MA: Harvard University Press.

ANSCOMBE, F. J. (1960). Rejection of outliers. *Technometrics, 2*, 123–147.

ANSCOMBE, F. J. (1961). Examination of residuals. *Proceedings of the Fourth Berkeley Symposium on Mathematical Statistics and Probability*. Berkeley: University of California Press.

BAKER, R. J., & NELDER, J. A. (1978). *GLIM manual, Release 3*. Oxford: Numerical Algorithms Group and Royal Statistical Society.

BALDUS, D. C., & COLE, J. W. L. (1980). *Statistical proof of discrimination*. New York: McGraw Hill.

BARNDORFF-NIELSEN, O. (1978). *Information and exponential families in statistical theory*. New York: Wiley.

BARNETT, V. (1973). *Comparative statistical inference*. New York: Wiley.

BECKER, W. E., & BAUMOL, W. J. (Eds.). (1996). *Assessing educational practices: the contribution of economics*. Cambridge: MIT Press.

BENNET, J. E., RACINE-POON, A., & WAKEFIELD, J. C. (1996). MCMC for nonlinear hierarchical models. In W. R. Gilks, S. Richardson, & D. J. Spiegelhalter (Eds.), *Markov Monte Carlo in Practice*. London: Chapman & Hall.

BIRNBAUM, A. (1962). On the foundations of statistical inference (with Discussion). *Journal of the American Statistical Association, 57*, 269–306.

BISHOP, Y. M. M., FIENBERG, S. E., & HOLLAND, P. W. (1975). *Discrete Multivariate Analysis: Theory and Practice.* Cambridge, MA: MIT Press.

BOYD, W. L. (1998). Productive schools from a policy perspective. In W. T. Hartman & W. L. Boyd (Eds.). *Resource allocation and productivity in education: Theory and practice.* (pp. 1–22). Westport, CN: Greenwood Press.

BOYD, W. L., & HARTMAN, W. T. (1998). The politics of educational productivity. In W. T. Hartman & W. L. Boyd (Eds.). *Resource allocation and productivity in education: Theory and practice.* (pp. 23–56). Westport, CN: Greenwood Press.

BRADLEY, R. A., & GART, J. J. (1962). The asymptotic properties of ML estimators when sampling from associated populations. *Biometrika, 49,* 205–214.

BRESLOW, N. E., & CLAYTON, D. G. (1993). Approximate inference in generalized linear mixed models. *Journal of the American Statistical Association, 88,* 9–25.

BROWN, M. B., & FUCHS, C. (1983). On maximum likelihood estimation in sparse contingency tables. *Computational Statistics and Data Analysis, 1,* 3–15.

BUONACCORSI, J. P. (1996). Measurement error in the response in the general linear model. *Journal of the American Statistical Association, 91,* 633–642.

CARLIN, B. P., & LOUIS, T. A. (1996). *Bayes and empirical Bayes methods for data analysis.* New York: Chapman & Hall.

CASELLA, G., & BERGER, R. L. (1990). *Statistical inference.* Pacific Grove, CA: Wadsworth & Brooks/Cole.

COOK, P., & BROEMELING, L. D. (1994). A Bayesian WLS approach to generalized linear models. *Communications in Statistics: Theory Methods Methods, 23,* 3323–3347.

COX, D. R., & SNELL, E. J. (1968). A general definition of residuals. *Journal of the Royal Statistical Society. Series B, 30,* 248–265.

DANIELS, M. J., & GATSONIS, C. (1999). Hierarchical generalized linear models in the analysis of variations in healthcare utilization. *Journal of the American Statistical Association, 94,* 29–42.

DEGROOT, M. H. (1986). *Probability and statistics.* Reading, MA: Addison-Wesley.

DEL PINO, G. (1989). The unifying role of iterative generalized least squares in statistical algorithms. *Statistical Science, 4,* 394–408.

DOBSON, A. J. (1990). *An introduction to generalized linear models.* New York: Chapman & Hall.

EFRON, B. (1986). Double exponential families and their use in generalized linear regression. *Journal of the American Statistical Association, 81,* 709–721.

FAHRMEIR, L., & KAUFMAN, H. (1985). Consistency and asymptotic normality of the maximum likelihood estimator in generalized linear models. *The Annals of Statistics, 13,* 342–368.

FAHRMEIR, L., & TUTZ, G. (1994). *Multivariate statistical modelling based on generalized linear models.* New York: Springer-Verlag.

FISHER, R. A. (1922). On the mathematical foundations of theoretical statistics. *Philosophical Transactions of the Royal Statistical Society of London A, 222,* 309–360.

FISHER, R. A. (1925). Theory of statistical estimation. *Proceedings of the Cambridge Philosophical Society, 22,* 700–725.

FISHER, R. A. (1934). Two new properties of mathematical likelihood. *Proceedings of the Royal Society A*, *144*, 285–307.

GHOSH, M., NATARAJAN, K., STROUD, T. W. F., & CARLIN, B. P. (1998). Generalized linear models for small-area estimation. *Journal of the American Statistical Association*, *93*, 273–282.

GILL, J. (1999). The insignificance of null hypothesis significance testing. *Political Research Quarterly*, *52*, 647–674.

GOOD, I. J. (1986). Saturated model or quasimodel: A point of terminology. *Journal of Statistical Computation and Simulation*, *24*, 168–169.

GREEN, P. J. (1984). Iteratively reweighted least squares for maximum likelihood estimation, and some robust and resistant alternatives. *Journal of the Royal Statistical Society, Series B*, *46*, 149–192.

GREENE, W. (1997). *Econometric analysis* (3rd ed.). New York: Prentice Hall.

GREENE, W. (2000). *Econometric analysis* (4th ed.). New York: Prentice Hall.

GREENWALD, A. G. (1975). Consequences of prejudice against the null hypothesis. *Psychological Bulletin*, *82*, 1–20.

HANUSHEK, E. A. (1981). Throwing money at schools. *Journal of Policy Analysis and Management*, *1*, 19–41.

HANUSHEK, E. A. (1986). The economics of schooling: production and efficiency in public schools. *Journal of Economic Literature*, *24*, 1141–1177.

HANUSHEK, E. A. (1994). Money might matter somewhere: A response to Hedges, Laine, and Greenwald. *Educational Researcher*, *23*, 5–8.

HÄRDLE, W., MAMMEN, E., & MÜLLER, M. (1988). Testing parametric versus semiparametric modeling in generalized linear models. *Journal of the American Statistical Association*, *89*, 501–511.

HARVEY, A. (1989). *Forecasting, statistical time series models and the Kalman filter.* Cambridge: Cambridge University Press.

HARVEY, A., & KOOPMAN, S. J. (1993). Forecasting hourly electricity demand using time-varying splines. *Journal of the American Statistical Association*, *88*, 1228–1236.

HASTIE, T. J., & TIBSHIRANI, R. J. (1990). *Generalized additive models.* New York: Chapman & Hall.

HASTIE, T. J., & TIBSHIRANI, R. J. (1993). Varying-coefficient models. *Journal of the Royal Statistical Society, Series B*, *55*, 757–796.

HEDGES, L. V., LAINE, R. D. & GREENWALD, R. (1994). Does money matter? A meta-analysis of studies of the effects of differential school inputs on student outcomes. *Educational Researcher*, *23*, 383–393.

IBRAHIM, J. G., & LAUD, P. W. (1991). On Bayesian analysis of generalized linear models using Jeffreys' prior. *Journal of the American Statistical Association*, *86*, 981–986.

JØRGENSEN, B. (1983). Maximum likelihood estimation and large-sample inference for generalized linear and nonlinear regression models. *Biometrics*, *70*, 19–28.

KASS, R. E. (1993). Bayes factors in practice. *The Statistician*, *42*, 551–560.

KAUFMAN, H. (1987). Regression models for nonstationary categorical time series: Asymptotic estimation theory. *Annals of Statistics*, *15*, 79–98.

KING, G. (1989). *Unifying political methodology: The likelihood theory of statistical inference*. Cambridge: Cambridge University Press.

KLEPPNER, D., & RAMSEY, N. (1985). *Quick calculus: A self-teaching guide*. New York: Wiley Self Teaching Guides.

KOEHLER, A. B., & MURPHREE, E. S. (1988). A comparison of the Akaike and Schwarz criteria for selecting model order. *Applied Statistics*, 187–195.

KRZANOWSKI, W. J. (1988). *Principles of multivariate analysis*. Oxford: Clarendon Press.

LEAMER, E. E. (1978). *Specification searches: Ad hoc inference with nonexperimental data*. New York: Wiley.

LE CAM, L., & YANG, G. L. (1990). *Asymptotics in statistics: Some basic concepts*. New York: Springer-Verlag.

LEHMANN, E. L., & CASELLA, G. (1998). *Theory of point estimation* (2nd ed.). New York: Springer-Verlag.

LIANG, K. Y., & ZEGER, S. L. (1986). Longitudinal analysis using generalized linear models. *Biometrika*, *73*, 13–22.

LINDSAY, R. M. (1995). Reconsidering the status of tests of significance: An alternative criterion of adequacy. *Accounting, Organizations and Society*, *20*, 35–53.

LINDSEY, J. K. (1997). *Applying generalized linear models*. New York: Springer-Verlag.

MAURICE, S. C., & SMITHSON, C. W. (1985). *Managerial economics: Applied microeconomics for decision making*. Homewood, IL: Irwin.

McCULLAGH, P. (1983). Quasi-likelihood functions. *The Annals of Statistics*, *11*, 59–67.

McCULLAGH, P., & Nelder, J. A. (1989). *Generalized linear models*. (2nd ed.). New York: Chapman & Hall.

McCULLOCH, C. E. (1997). Maximum likelihood algorithms for generalized linear mixed models. *Journal of the American Statistical Association*, *92*, 162–170.

McGILCHRIST, C. A. (1994). Estimation in generalized mixed models. *Journal of the Royal Statistical Society, Series B*, *55*, 945–955.

MEIER, K. J., STEWART, J., Jr., & ENGLAND, R. E. (1991). The politics of bureaucratic discretion: Education access as an urban service. *American Journal of Political Science*, *35(1)*, 155–177.

MILLER, A. J. (1990). *Subset selection in regression*. New York: Chapman & Hall.

MURNANE, R. J. (1975). *The impact of school resources on the learning of inner city children*. Cambridge: Ballinger Press.

NAYLOR, J. C., & SMITH, A. F. M. (1982). Applications of a method for the efficient computation of posterior distributions. *Applied Statistics*, *31*, 214–225.

NEFTÇI, S. N. (1982). Specification of economic time series models using Akaike's criterion. *Journal of the American Statistical Association*, *77*, 537–540.

NELDER, J. A., & PREGIBON, D. (1987). An extended quasi-likelihood function. *Biometrika*, *74*, 221–232.

NELDER, J. A., & WEDDERBURN, R. W. M. (1972). Generalized linear models. *Journal of the Royal Statistical Society, Series A*, *135*, 370–385.

98

NETER, J., KUTNER, M. H., NACHTSHEIM, C. J., & WASSERMAN, W. (1996). *Applied linear regression models*. Chicago: Irwin.

NORDBERG, L. (1980). Asymptotic normality of maximum likelihood estimators based on independent unequally distributed observation in exponential family models. *Scandinavian Journal of Statistics*, 7, 27–32.

PEERS, H. W. (1971). Likelihood ratio and associated test criteria. *Biometrika*, 58, 577–589.

PIERCE, D. A., & SCHAFER, D. W. (1986). Residuals in generalized linear models. *Journal of the American Statistical Society*, 81, 977–986.

PREGIBON, D. (1981). Logistic regression diagnostics. *The Annals of Statistics*, 9, 705–724.

PREGIBON, D. (1984). Review of generalized linear models by McCullagh and Nelder. *American Statistician*, 12, 1589–1596.

QUINLAN, C. (1987). *Year-round education, year-round opportunities: A study of year-round education in California*. Sacramento: California State Department of Education.

RAFTERY, A. E. (1995). Bayesian model selection in social research. In P. V. Marsden, (Ed.). *Sociological Methodology*. (pp. 111–195). Cambridge, MA: Blackwells.

ROZEBOOM, W. W. (1960). The fallacy of the null hypothesis significance test. *Psychological Bulletin*, 57, 416–428.

SAWA, T. (1978). Information criteria for discriminating among alternative regression models. *Econometrica*, 46, 1273–1291.

SCHWARZ, G. (1978). Estimating the dimension of a model. *Annals of Statistics*, 6, 461–464.

SEVERINI, T. A., & STANISWALIS, J. G. (1994). Quasi-likelihood estimation in semi-parametric models. *Journal of the American Statistical Association*, 89, 501–511.

SU, J. Q., & WEI, L. J. (1991). A lack-of-fit test for the mean function in a generalized linear model. *Journal of the American Statistical Association*, 86, 420–426.

THEOBALD, N., & GILL, J. (1999). Looking for data in all the wrong places: An analysis of California's STAR results. *Paper presented at the Annual Meeting of the Western Political Science Association, Seattle, WA, March*. Available at http://web.clas.ufl.edu/~jgill.

UPTON, G. J. G. (1991). The exploratory analysis of survey data using log-linear models. *The Statistician*, 40, 169–182.

WALKER, S. G., & MALLICK, B. K. (1997). Hierarchical generalized linear models and frailty models with Bayesian nonparametric mixing. *Journal of the Royal Statistical Society, Series B*, 59, 845–860.

WANG, N., LIN, X., GUTIERREZ, R. G., & CARROLL, R. J. (1998). Bias analysis and SIMEX approach in generalized linear mixed measurement error models. *Journal of the American Statistical Association*, 93, 249–261.

WEAVER, T. (1992). Year-round education. *ERIC Digest*, 68, ED342107.

WEDDERBURN, R. W. M. (1974). Quasi-likelihood functions, generalized linear models, and the Gauss–Newton method. *Biometrika*, 61, 439–447.

WEDDERBURN, R. W. M. (1976). On the existence and uniqueness of the maximum likelihood estimates for certain generalized linear models. *Biometrika, 63*, 27–32.

WEST, M., HARRISON, P. J., & MIGON, H. S. (1985). Dynamic generalized linear models and Bayesian forecasting. *Journal of the American Statistical Association, 80*, 73–83.

WIRT, F. M., & KIRST, M. W. (1975). *Political and social foundations of education.* Berkeley: McCutchan.

WOLFINGER, R., & O'CONNELL, M. (1993). Generalized linear mixed models: A pseudolikelihood approach. *Journal of Statistical Computation and Simulation, 48*, 233–243.

ZEGER, S. L., & KARIM, R. (1991). Generalized linear models with random effects; A Gibbs sampling approach. *Journal of the American Statistical Association, 86*, 79–86.

ZEGER, S. L., & LIANG, K. Y. (1986). Longitudinal data analysis for discrete and continuous outcomes. *Biometrics, 42*, 121–130.

ZELLNER, A., & ROSSI, P. E. (1984). Bayesian analysis of dichotomous quantal response models. *Journal of Econometrics, 25*, 365–393.

ZHANG, P. (1992). On the distributional properties of model selection. *Journal of the American Statistical Association, 87*, 732–737.

# ABOUT THE AUTHOR

*JEFF GILL* is Assistant Professor of Political Science at the University of Florida. He received his Ph.D. from American University in 1996, studying both political science and mathematical statistics. His primary research applies Bayesian modeling and data analysis to substantive questions in public policy, budgeting, bureaucracy, voting behavior, and Congress. His work has appeared previously in *Public Administration Review*, in *Political Research Quarterly*, as well as with Georgetown University Press, Brookings Institution Press, and others. He has recently published a methodology book with Ken Meier titled *What Works: A New Approach to Program and Policy Analysis.*